12/16/20
15.99

In *Raising Up Dreamers*, Shelia gives us an incredible guide and set of tools to help develop our children into all God has designed them to be. Through her own experience raising her sons, my friends and business partners Andy and Jon Erwin, Shelia shares the wisdom she has gained in various seasons of parenting to show us that our goal as parents should be to help our children know Jesus and make Him known. As a father of three sons, I recognize the responsibility my wife and I have in doing this. Through *Raising Up Dreamers*, we now have more tools to help raise our children to fulfill God's destiny for each of their lives. If you're a parent or hope to be one someday, this book is a treasure trove of wisdom and will be sure to benefit anyone who reads it!

KEVIN DOWNES, co-CEO of Kingdom Story Company; producer, actor, director, and writer

I believe some people are born with a creative spark, but I also believe it has to be fanned into a flame. I have watched Andy and Jon Erwin as their spark became a roaring fire touching the lives of millions. *Raising Up Dreamers* provides much-needed parental insights and practical tips for raising up your dreamers.

MIKE CALHOUN, pastor of ministry training, The Summit Church, Raleigh, NC

I have worked closely with Andrew and Jon Erwin over the past ten years, so much so that I'm often referred to as the "third Erwin brother." As we've made films and built a business together, I've constantly been impressed at the example of Andy and Jon, their brother bond, the way they work as a team, their respect for each other, and how they seek to resolve conflicts. This is, no doubt, a direct result of the intentional parenting style of Hank and Shelia Erwin. In *Raising Up Dreamers*, Shelia writes about the ways she cultivated these skills in her sons while teaching them to love the Lord and encouraging them to always dream bigger.

JOSHUA WALSH, president, Kingdom S
Entertainment

D1489114

I *love* this book! This is truly a book that every mother and father needs to read. This book will help the reader raise godly men and women into their calling. We as parents have the ability to help shape our children to walk in their God-given purpose, helping them to keep their eyes focused on Christ while living passionate, creative lives for Jesus!

> **SHARI RIGBY,** actress, *October Baby, Overcomer*; speaker; author of *Beautifully Flawed*; director and founder of "The Women in My World"

I wish this book had been available to me when I was raising my children! It's written so you can read it straight through, or as a situational reference guide to help your children navigate challenging situations. *Raising Up Dreamers* is a true gift for all parents!

> **ANN BARROWS,** widow of Cliff Barrows, Billy Graham's longtime musical director

This is an outstanding book about parenting, about how to help our children discover the dreams God has for them, and about what we can do as parents to help them realize those dreams. But more than that, it's a book about life. We can recommend it to you without reservation. Read and be blessed!

> **BRYAN FISCHER,** author of *The Boy to Man Book*; former chaplain of the Idaho State Senate; host of *Focal Point* on the American Family Radio talk network

Raising Up Dreamers is an incredible resource, filled with biblical wisdom for raising your kids to be all that God has purposed and planned for them to be. I've heard it said that parenting doesn't come with a manual—well, it does now. So wherever you are in the journey of raising your kids, you'll be encouraged to finish well.

> **KEITH LOY,** senior pastor, Celebrate Community Church, Sioux Falls, SD, and **KAY LOY,** homeschool mom

Like fresh manna from heaven, *Raising Up Dreamers* is an amazing and insightful guide that every parent and grandparent will want in their family's toolbox! We were riveted by the parenting experiences Shelia transparently revealed, both the good and the challenging. Her sound wisdom and advice are laid out in such a way that it's simple and easy to follow. These tips and tools are the "proverbs of parenting," whether you're in the valley and feeling overwhelmed or on the mountaintop enjoying a smooth season. It's truly refreshing to finally have a book that offers practical teachings and detailed advice with a rock-solid foundation! We believe *Raising Up Dreamers* will empower and motivate parents to inspire their children to be all they can be, as surely as God has created them.

DAVID SCHMIDT, aviation director and pilot for Samaritan's Purse, and **NATALIE SCHMIDT,** homeschool mom, women's Bible study teacher, and certified crisis intervention chaplain

Raising Up Dreamers teaches parents how to pour God's Word into the hearts of their children and then inspire them to pursue the dreams He gives them. Lorie and I have been friends with Hank and Shelia Erwin for over twenty years. They have graciously poured into us the tips and tools discussed in this book as we have been raising our four guys. The principles are sound and engage the heart of the child—they don't just focus on behavior. I recommend that *all* dads and moms read this book.

JOHN KIRKLAND, former president of North Carolinians for Home Education

Raising Up Dreamers is a very easy read that gives practical application to the deep truths of Scripture. This is a great tool to help parents teach and train in righteousness and encourage their children to pursue their God-given dreams.

LORIE KIRKLAND, mom of four grown homeschooled dreamers

As a mother, Shelia knew that a connection with God was a gift that wouldn't limit the size of Andy and Jon's dreams. I trust that reading this book will inspire all of us to make a difference in our lives by listening to God's whispers and to "raise up dreamers" too.

EDIE HAND, international speaker, author, filmmaker; voice of "Women of True Grit" on *Our American Stories*; and mom who raised a dreamer

What a timeless book, filled with nuggets of gold and godly advice for all parents, as well as grandparents. *Raising Up Dreamers* is for those who truly want to focus on raising godly children for their generation who always dream their God-given dreams.

PATSY RILEY, former First Lady of the 52nd governor of Alabama (Bob Riley)

This book is a biography, a gospel story, a Bible study, and a parenting manual all in one. When I think of the Erwin Brothers, I think of accomplished professionals making a difference for God in the marketplace of cinema, but the book explains every step in getting to the place where God took their talent and training and made it a force for His message of the gospel.

TOM PHILLIPS, pastor, New Heights Baptist Church, Ringgold, GA

Raising Up Dreamers

Raising Up DREAMERS

Find and Grow Your Child's God-Given Talents

Shelia Erwin

Tyndale House Publishers
Carol Stream, Illinois

FOCUS ON THE FAMILY®

Raising Up Dreamers: Find and Grow Your Child's God-Given Talents
© 2020 Shelia Erwin. All rights reserved.

A Focus on the Family book published by Tyndale House Publishers, Carol Stream, Illinois 60188

Focus on the Family and the accompanying logo and design are federally registered trademarks of Focus on the Family, 8605 Explorer Drive, Colorado Springs, CO 80920.

TYNDALE and Tyndale's quill logo are registered trademarks of Tyndale House Publishers.

No part of this publication may be reproduced, stored in a retrieval system, or transmitted in any form or by any means—electronic, mechanical, photocopy, recording, or otherwise—without prior written permission of Focus on the Family.

All Scripture quotations, unless otherwise marked, are from the Amplified® Bible [paraphrase], Classic Edition, copyright © 1954, 1958, 1962, 1964, 1965, 1987 by The Lockman Foundation. Used by permission. (www.Lockman.org). Scripture quotations marked (AMP) are taken from the Amplified® Bible [paraphrase], copyright © 2015 by The Lockman Foundation. Used by permission. (www.Lockman.org). Scripture quotations marked (ASV) are taken from *The Holy Bible*, American Standard Version. Scripture quotations marked (ESV) are from *The Holy Bible, English Standard Version.* Copyright © 2001 by CrosswayBibles, a publishing ministry of Good News Publishers. Used by permission. All rights reserved. Scripture quotations marked (KJV) are taken from the *Holy Bible*, King James Version. Scripture quotations marked (NASB) are taken from the *New American Standard Bible®*. Copyright © 1960, 1962, 1963, 1968, 1971, 1972, 1973, 1975, 1977, 1995 by The Lockman Foundation. Used by permission. (www.Lockman.org). Scripture quotations marked (TLB) are taken from *The Living Bible* [paraphrase], copyright © 1971 by Tyndale House Foundation. Used by permission of Tyndale House Publishers, Carol Stream, Illinois 60188. All rights reserved.

Cover design by Kim Reid

The use of material from or references to various websites does not imply endorsement of those sites in their entirety. Availability of websites and pages is subject to change without notice.

The author is represented by the literary agency of Wolgemuth & Associates.

For information about special discounts for bulk purchases, please contact Tyndale House Publishers at csresponse@tyndale.com, or call 1-800-323-9400.

ISBN 978-1-58997-999-4

Printed in the United States of America

26	25	24	23	22	21	20
7	6	5	4	3	2	1

3 4873 00565 6863

There are so many people who have truly invested in my walk with the Lord, and to all of you I am grateful! But there is only one person to whom I can dedicate this book, and that is Mrs. Joyce Yancey. Since September 1972 she has invested her life into my life, as my "spiritual mom and mentor." So much of who I am comes from our relationship.

My friends started to call me "Echo," because when I opened my mouth, so much of what Joyce was teaching came out of me. Watching her walk with the Lord through some very hard times grew my faith and trust in the Lord. Much of what is in this book came from this relationship.

With a heart filled with gratitude, I dedicate this book to you, dear sweet Joyce. It has been a pleasure to be your "echo." Thank you for seeing that twenty-three-year-old young woman's heart and for being such a big part of who I am today. Thank you for your passion for Scripture and your love for the living Word of God (Jesus).

CONTENTS

Foreword xiii

Introduction: Dreams Do Come True xix

PART ONE: TIPS

TIP 1: Raise the Children God Has Given You 3

TIP 2: Teach Them about Their Uniqueness 7

TIP 3: Bring Them to Jesus 11

TIP 4: You Are the Right Mom 15

TIP 5: You Can Do Hard Things 21

TIP 6: Whose Dream Is It? 25

TIP 7: They Are Lent to You 29

TIP 8: Discipline Your Children 35

TIP 9: God Enables You 49

TIP 10: Join in the Fun and Be Their Fan 57

TIP 11: Teach about Disappointment 63

TIP 12: Make Daily Deposits 69

TIP 13: Teach Them to Value Others 75

PART TWO: FOUNDATIONS

FOUNDATION 1: Watch and Learn 85

FOUNDATION 2: "Any Old Bush Will Do" 89

FOUNDATION 3: Recognize "But God" Moments 93

PART THREE: ESSENTIALS

ESSENTIAL 1: Embrace Your Faith 103

ESSENTIAL 2: Make Jesus Your Standard 107

ESSENTIAL 3: Follow the Supreme Authority 111

ESSENTIAL 4: Live Holy 115

ESSENTIAL 5: Fight the Dream Killers 127

ESSENTIAL 6: Find Power for Living 141

ESSENTIAL 7: Don't Do It Alone 153

PART FOUR: TOOLS

      TOOL 1: Submit to Authority 157

      TOOL 2: Dare Them to Be a Daniel 161

      TOOL 3: Cultivate Good Attitudes 167

      TOOL 4: Keep a Clean Heart 171

      TOOL 5: Deal with Conflict 173

      TOOL 6: Learn to Love 179

      TOOL 7: Learn to Pray 183

      TOOL 8: Be Armed for Battle 201

      TOOL 9: Life Is a Great Adventure 213

      TOOL 10: Give God Your Yes 217

Acknowledgments 227

Notes 229

FOREWORD

I REMEMBER WAKING UP one morning as a seven-year-old kid and my mom excitedly calling me into the garage. We didn't have a lot of money in those days for the big *Star Wars* play sets that I would scour the Toys "R" Us catalogs for.

My grandmother would enter the Publishers Clearing House sweepstakes every year and promise me that if she won, she would give me a hundred bucks to go on my shopping spree to help me finish telling my own story of the Rebel Alliance. But the sweepstakes never panned out as I hoped, much to my disappointment.

So my mom decided to take matters into her own hands. That morning I walked into our garage and onto the set of the most wonderful piece of maternal storytelling I have ever seen or heard of. The culmination of weeks of hard work was truly amazing. Shelia Erwin became a mom legend that day.

She had taken two sawhorses and two very large pieces of plywood, and on them had started re-creating every world from the films I loved so much. With Styrofoam, she had carved out the ice planet Hoth. With moss and roots, she had created Yoda's swamp, and with twigs and branches, she had meticulously re-created the Ewok village. I was stunned. I ran straight to my room and grabbed every action figure I had and set about finishing the story I'd daydreamed about for so long. In the weeks that followed, Jon, Mom, and I worked to finish this wonderful creation.

I think what my mom did that I appreciate to this day was this: She didn't just buy me another toy—she went far beyond that to engage with my imagination. For me, that was one of the first seeds of storytelling that was planted in my development. In that, I found my life's calling as a storyteller.

I'm grateful for parents who encouraged that kind of dreaming, who realized that serving God could be out of the box and creative. The Christian life was always framed for us as "the great adventure." I didn't realize it as a kid, but now, as an adult with children of my own, I see how many things my mom intentionally fostered in our lives that allowed us to find our purpose. I think she recognized the differences in each of her kids and allowed Jon and me to find our unique callings as creatives and as people.

I'm thrilled she's able to tell her side of the story now. My hope is that the words she writes in this book will encourage moms and help them realize the tremendous impact they can have on their children to dream big. I hope this book will motivate moms to inspire their kids to use their God-given talents in ways they never thought possible. *Raising Up Dreamers* isn't about making more filmmakers—it's about raising children in a home where it's safe for them to give their imaginations over to God and see what He will create through one little life.

Andrew Erwin

"DREAM BOLD. DREAM BIG. Dream the impossible." This statement echoed through the halls of the Erwin family household. This statement drove my brother, Andy, and me to chase after what others would deem unrealistic and illogical. This statement would catalyze the ambition needed to pull off the number one independent movie of 2018.

That's probably not what the first-grade teacher thought when she suspected I had ADHD and talked to my mom about it. They decided to put me back in kindergarten, and I stayed at that school through first grade. But Mom saw that my needs were not being met in a traditional classroom with its many distractions. My mother, an artistic, determined dreamer, didn't see me the way that school did. Where others saw a hyperactive eight-year-old, she instead saw burning creativity. She knew I needed to learn in my own way. Her instinct? She took me home to school and never looked back.

My mom's choice to homeschool me changed the trajectory of my life. For the first time, I wasn't berated for what I didn't have. Instead, we celebrated who I was. ADHD was no longer a hindrance but the key to a creative mind. My mother encouraged me to follow my innovative instincts and formed our lessons around them. Her school operated in a different way from the classic way of learning. Each day started off with thirty minutes of prayer. Granted, I could barely close my eyes for thirty seconds, but I learned the importance of prayer at an early age. My mother was not only a teacher of math, science, history, and the like. She was a teacher of faith.

Our family's life was always steeped in faith. Shades Mountain Independent Church, where my parents were heavily involved, was like a second home to me. This place became the foundation for everything I knew about God, and it was my mom who first led me to Christ. I'll never forget that day in our ugly, beat-up station wagon when she listened to my questions and walked me through salvation. From that day on, my parents never failed to strengthen my belief in God, as well as my belief in myself.

My parents' philosophy on life is that God has given each of us talents for a divine purpose larger than ourselves. They instilled this in us from the moment we could walk. Dreams were not something far off in the distance; dreams were our destiny. God has a plan, so why not chase your passions? Our parents were unwavering supporters of my brother and me as we pursued film. They used money they didn't have to buy us our first camera, drove us to our first jobs, helped us get a loan for equipment—the list of their support is endless. They believed in us wholeheartedly, especially in our moments of doubt.

The path to success demands failure, and my mom and dad gave us the opportunity to fail. We never would have learned anything without the room to make mistakes. They also let us go into the world of entertainment without sheltering us from the chaos. Their goal for us was to be capable adults rather than good children, and they allowed experiences that showed us how to stand firm in our faith and identity. They let God use us where He wanted to, despite the evil that sometimes surrounds the entertainment industry. If they hadn't done that, there's no way Andy and I would be able to be an influencing voice of faith in film.

To those of you reading this book, I want to encourage you to adopt the same radical belief in your children that my parents had in us. The Lord has gifted your children, and they have a unique destiny. You can help draw those gifts out of them. Relentlessly frustrating kids often have insane, astronomically sized dreams, and they're just waiting for someone to believe in who they are.

As I've started my own parenting journey, I've taken so much joy in trying to nurture my kids' biggest dreams. Every kid wants to do big things, and life has a way of stifling that. It's our job as parents to remind them that God can take something that seems truly impossible and bring it to fruition. And this book can show you what that looks like. Dream bold. Dream big. Dream the impossible.

Jon Erwin

INTRODUCTION

Dreams Do Come True

*Now unto him that is able to do exceeding abundantly above
all that we ask or think, according to the power that worketh in us, unto
him be glory in the church by Christ Jesus throughout all ages,
world without end. Amen. (Ephesians 3:20-21, KJV)*

IT WAS 8:00 A.M. on April 30, 2014, and my husband, Hank, and I were standing with our arms around each other looking out our hotel window at Grauman's Chinese Theatre.

As we gazed out our window at the street in front of the theater below, we giggled like two children on Christmas morning.

"This is really cool!" I said.

It was one of those "worth it" moments for us as parents. You see, later that night we would be stepping over the footprints of some of Hollywood's elite as we walked the red carpet with our sons and their wives for the world premiere of their movie *Moms' Night Out*.

Hank quickly got dressed and headed down to the theater to meet up with our sons, Andy and Jon. Together, they watched while the huge movie poster was lifted forty feet in the air to the top of the theater's entrance and the wide red carpet rolled out.

As I watched the activity below my window and saw them all having fun taking pictures with their cell phones and posting on Facebook, I began to reflect on the adventure that had brought us here, to this day.

Since we'd arrived in Los Angeles, we'd been asked so many questions about our sons. I was asked what I thought when Andy, then sixteen, and Jon, then twelve, announced, "We think God wants us to make movies someday."

I think one word would describe how I felt that day—*delight*. From that first day on, I truly believed that God had called my sons to create movies, and that somehow, He would make it happen. And I also believed that He had called me, as a mom, to be an important part of that process. You see, I've lived most of my life with a man (my husband) who believed, "Dream big, dream amazing, dream impossible, because life with Jesus is a great adventure." God has used Hank to teach me to live my great adventure and pass that on to our sons.

In this day and age, we moms are told that what we do is not important. We start to feel like failures; we feel weary and worn-out, frustrated and unfulfilled, guilty and shamed, jaded and exasperated, inadequate and incapable—just bad moms. At the same time, we're also told that we are not doing our part in contributing to society.

I've written this book to share my journey with you, my adventure of being the mom to two extremely creative men, and I want to encourage you in your journey. What you are doing—whether you're a mom working outside your home, a stay-at-home mom, or a homeschool mom—is important. Investing your life in the lives of your children is always worthwhile. At the end of *Moms' Night Out*, Sean (played by actor Sean Astin) says, "What you do is important. . . . The hand that rocks the cradle is the hand that rules the world."[1] This quote is actually from a poem by William Ross Wallace in which he praises motherhood as the "preeminent force for change in the world."[2]

Two words that are so often found in Scripture have helped me with my adventure of raising up dreamers. The phrase "but God" shows us who God is and what He has done and will do for us. As we live and walk through this life, the "but God" moments in our walk are often a change of direction or a divine intervention. My life has been filled with many "but God" times that have truly led me to trust and have faith in Jesus Christ. My battle cry in the journey of raising up dreamers truly became "not I" (Mom) "but God" (Christ).

As moms, we can easily become discouraged as we wear many hats—especially those of us who have highly creative children. Through my stories of raising two successful filmmakers using biblical principles, which have given them the tools for the work God has called them to, I want to encourage you to cultivate your children's gifts and help them reach their dreams—no matter how impossible they may seem.

PART ONE

Tips

Finding and growing your child's God-given talents might sound a bit overwhelming. Here are a few tips that the Lord has taught me along the way about raising children to follow His calling.

TIP 1:

Raise the Children God Has Given You

LET ME INTRODUCE YOU to the two blessings that God has allowed me to co-parent.

I remember sitting in church and looking at my sons in an honest way. As I looked at Andy, my sweet-spirited firstborn, I saw tenderness, patience, kindness, and one who truly considers others. Yet he was a child given to self-pity and internalized anger, with unbelievable stubbornness and sneakiness. He had been a ten-month-old who, after being corrected for touching a plant, would crawl around to the back of that plant, hide, and wait until he thought no one was looking—and then touch the plant again. He had been a four-year-old who would stand stiff at the top of the stairs with his hands in fists, shaking with anger and saying, "I just want my own way!"

He was brilliant (I know all moms think that, but he really was). He started to talk at seven months, made sentences by one year, and was conversational by eighteen months. He started to read at two years old. By the age of three he could start with the letter *A* and recite a Bible verse for each letter of the alphabet.

He was a compliant child as well—at least until he turned four and we began to see his will.

As I looked at Jon, my happy, fun-loving secondborn, I saw a child who filled my life with laughter, who loved to perform for people, and thought *the more the merrier*. I saw a child who was creative, who could make something out of nothing. He was a child who would openly tell me, "No, I will not!" for hours on end. He wanted to be in control of everything and everyone around him. He was one who was given to outward anger, yet a child who was truly afraid of everything around him.

Jon was born prematurely by emergency C-section because of the loss of a heartbeat. We almost lost him that day. Jon came here full of laughter and confrontation. Even though it was obvious Jon also had a high IQ and a photographic memory, as a former educator, I quickly saw that there were areas in which he was struggling. After kindergarten, he was diagnosed with attention deficit hyperactivity disorder (ADHD).

I share this because I'm not asking you to do something I haven't already done. You see, I saw such wonderful traits unfolding in my sons' temperaments, yet at the same time, I saw character issues that if left unbridled would one day rise up and destroy them. I had been taught that it was my job to work hard on taming the wild stallion that is such a part of all of us. Natural bents left to run free would destroy my sons and hurt others around them and even destroy future generations. But if those same traits were brought under the control of the Master's hand, they could be useful and would be the making of wonderful thoroughbreds.

After an honest look at my sons, fear could have filled my

heart. Instead, I could hear Jesus speaking into it: "Shelia, bring the little children unto Me!" I began to learn that only Jesus could tame the inward man in my sons' hearts. I also knew that He had called me to be their mom, and I was to be used in their lives by God to begin the work of transformation. He reminded me of what He had said in James 1:5: "If any of you is deficient in wisdom, let him ask of the giving God [Who gives] to everyone liberally and ungrudgingly, without reproaching or faultfinding, and it will be given him." Wisdom would be freely given to me if I just asked. I prayed, "Here are my heart, my hands, my voice, and my mind. Please use me to parent my children, to bring them under your control, God." In my journey of motherhood, I asked for wisdom, and God provided. He taught me how to nurture curiosity, creativity, and compassion. He will do the same for you if you ask.

Teach Them about Their Uniqueness

CAN WE DEFINE THE CREATIVE CHILD? What does a creative child look like? Is there just one flavor? Is there just one area of giftedness? Is there only one formula that always has the same outcome? I believe that the answer to all those questions is no. If *creative* means the ability or capacity of someone to create or produce something, then every one of our children would fit into that description. It's not just talent, creative ability, or being a dreamer that defines a creative child, but also factors such as temperament (personality traits), environment, and spiritual gifts (see 1 Corinthians 12:4-5).

Remember, you're raising children, not robots. It takes a lot of time for you to study and know your children, to discover their unique characters, their gifts and talents, and then to teach them based on what you've learned.

I remember sitting down with my guys in their preteen years with Beverly LaHaye's book *Understanding Your Child's Temperament* and teaching them about how different we all are. They immediately recognized each other's temperament.

"So that's why you do the things you do," each said to the other.

That book also helped me know each of them better. I taught them about how the body of Christ functions and that we all have at least one spiritual motivational gift that is given to us at the time of our salvation. I believe these two things have helped them with filmmaking and with relationships both at home and at work.

I was a creative child myself, and I drove my mother up the wall. When I was about twelve years old, I spent many hours painting a portrait of my mom while she was in the hospital. On the day she arrived home, I met her at the door with my gift, but all she could see was the oil paint all over her kitchen table.

As a mom, I can now understand her displeasure with the mess. I realize now that our temperaments were different. We didn't see life the same way, and therefore our priorities in life weren't the same. But she was good for me. God used her to teach me to live a disciplined life and to not let the creative part of myself control and consume me. Yet my mom's lack of acknowledgment of my creative efforts that day was painful. As you deal with the negative traits of your creative child, try to see things through his or her eyes, not just your grown-up mommy eyes.

One of the most important things we need to know is that each of us is a unique creation of God. Psalm 139:14 says, "I praise you, for I am *fearfully* and *wonderfully made. Wonderful* are your works; my soul knows it very well" (ESV, emphasis added). The Word also tells us that the church—the body of Christ; His bride; all believers—is made up of living stones, not bricks. Bricks are all the same size, but stones are all unique.

I had a daily reminder of that truth where I used to live. It's a wonderful little community in Alabama, right outside the city of Birmingham, where most everything is built from stones. When I looked around at the walls and buildings, I was reminded of how different each stone is. They're varied in appearance, yet all fit together beautifully.

I have several lovely sets of fine china I like to use for dinner parties. And I have a set of pots and pans I use to cook our meals. I especially enjoy using my cast-iron skillet to cook corn bread in the oven. Is either the china or skillet better than the other? No. They're just different because they have different uses. What would happen to my fine china if I tried to use it to cook corn bread in the oven? And would I serve you dinner out of my skillet? Of course not. We are all distinctive, and so are our stories. What if we learned to live our life simply as God made us, with originality, not trying to copy someone else? We can still learn from another person's story, because we are told in Scripture to follow those who follow Him. However, we're to follow the way they walk, not attempt to become them. With a grand purpose in mind, God made only one of each of us. Let your children know that they are unique. They are fearfully and wonderfully made, and God has a unique plan for their uniqueness. Ask God to give them a clear understanding of the destiny He designed them to accomplish.

TIP 3:

Bring Them to Jesus

Do YOUR CHILDREN really know Jesus? If not, there are three things they need *to know* and only one thing they need *to do*.

Three Things They Need to Know

1. God loves us.

- "For God so greatly loved and dearly prized the world that He [even] gave up His only begotten (unique) Son, so that whoever believes in (trusts in, clings to, relies on) Him shall not perish (come to destruction, be lost) but have eternal (everlasting) life" (John 3:16).

2. Sin (rebellion toward God) entered into mankind through Adam and Eve and therefore caused a separation between all of us and the God who made us.

- The fall of man is shown in Genesis 3:1-6.

- Romans 3:23 says, "All have sinned and are falling short of the honor and glory which God bestows and receives."

3. Jesus Christ is God's only provision for our sin and way to relationship with God.

- The person of the Lord Jesus Christ is God, the Son: "And immediately in the synagogues he proclaimed Jesus, saying, He is the Son of God!" (Acts 9:20).

- The work of the Lord Jesus Christ is that He willingly died on the cross, shedding His blood as payment for our sin. He came back to life again and lives forevermore (see 1 Corinthians 15:3-4).

- "Jesus said to him, I am the Way and the Truth and the Life; no one comes to the Father except by (through) Me" (John 14:6).

One Thing They Need to Do
Receive Jesus Christ as Savior.

- Man's responsibility: "But to as many as did receive and welcome Him, He gave the authority (power, privilege, right) to become the children of God, that is, to those who believe in (adhere to, trust in, and rely on) His name" (John 1:12).

- Admit that you are a sinner and that you desire to turn from your sin (repent).

- Believe that Jesus died for your sins and that you must receive Him through faith:
  - "For it is by free grace (God's unmerited favor) that you are saved (delivered from judgment and made partakers of Christ's salvation) through [your] faith. And this [salvation] is not of yourselves [of your own doing, it came not through your own striving], but it is the gift of God; not because of works [not the fulfillment of the Law's demands], lest any man should boast. [It is not the result of what anyone can possibly do, so no one can pride himself in it or take glory to himself]" (Ephesians 2:8-9).
  - Call on God in prayer, receiving Him by faith: "I am the Door; anyone who enters in through Me will be saved (will live). He will come in and he will go out [freely], and will find pasture" (John 10:9).

Do you *know* Him? Have you ever really understood that because of sin you are separated from God? Have you ever understood that Jesus became your substitute and took your punishment on the cross? Have you ever accepted His gift of salvation? Do you know that you are heaven-bound? Will you make sure right now?

Here's a suggested prayer: "Lord Jesus Christ, I admit that I'm a sinner, and I want to turn from my sin. I believe that You are the Son of God who died for my sin and that You are the One who can forgive me and take away my sin. I now receive You as my personal Savior. Amen."

When you become a Christ follower, you acquire His record

and His righteousness. You are a part of the family of God forever. This is the most important step you and your child can make.

Not only have I had the joy of leading my sons to Christ, but I've had the unspeakable joy of seeing them lead their own children to Christ as well.

The journey has to start with Jesus!

TIP 4:

You Are the Right Mom

TURN THE CLOCK BACK thirty-two years. I want to invite you into my world. Let me pour you a cup of coffee or tea and invite you to take a seat at my kitchen table.

Andy, eight, is not home right now, but Jon, my four-year-old ADHD bundle of willpower and creative energy, walks into the room where you and I are visiting. He is bored, and this is not a good thing. I can see it on his face because his eyebrows are moving up and down. This means his brain is brimming with imaginative impulses. Because I'm his mother, I know that soon there will be a sudden strong and reflexive urge to act.

This may be a good thing but maybe not.

Knowing the signs so well, I excuse myself, get up from the table, and hurry to my craft area to pick up a few things for him to use to ply his creativity while I'm chatting with you.

Soon I return with a handful of straws, paper clips, scissors, construction paper, several clear plastic cups, glue, tape, markers, and a shoebox.

"So sorry for the interruption," I say to you. But keeping

Jon occupied with something other than watching mindless cartoons is an important part of my day.

I call him over and tell him to look at my face as I'm speaking. Then I show him all the wonderful things I've collected for him to be creative with and instruct him to see what he can make from these treasures.

As you and I continue talking, Jon sets up shop on the floor close by. He's hard at work for about an hour. He then stands and shows us a robot, with cups for feet and legs that move up and down as he walks. Not bad for a four-year-old!

Of course, cleaning up the bits that remain on the floor will be his and mine to do. But to be sure, this was pure joy for the mother of a creative. A dreamer.

If I had known my sons were going to be so well-known one day, I would have kept that robot or at least have taken a picture of it, along with other myriad things Jon and Andy built over the years.

But not all of their creative ideas were good. Or safe. The trash can and the pool would fall into that category. We were blessed to have an in-ground pool when Andy and Jon were growing up, so they learned to swim at a young age. Because I could see the pool from almost every room in the house and with the windows open I could hear them, they were allowed to play in the water without me sitting out there.

One morning, when they were about seven and eleven years old, they came running into the house, dripping wet, asking me to come see their new pool trick. As I walked outside, Andy was strapping on his weight belt (they had been taking scuba lessons with their dad). He then put a trash can over his head and walked to the deep end and jumped in.

Alarmed, I shouted and ordered him out of the pool. He told me that there was an air pocket inside the trash can and that he could still breathe under there. After I gathered my composure, my son and I had a talk about the dangers of what he and his brother were doing and that they shouldn't do it again.

I've been asked one question numerous times: "Is there anything you would have done differently in parenting your sons?"

"There are only two things I would change," I've answered. "I would have been the perfect mother, and I would have had two perfect children." And then I laughed!

Elisabeth Elliot wrote, "The process of shaping the child . . . shapes also the mother herself. Reverence for her sacred burden calls her to all that is pure and good, that she may teach primarily by her own humble, daily example."[1]

One of my lifelong friends and I were talking about the subject of our mommy failures. Some were hard and some were just funny. I'm not so sure if they were funny at the time, but at least they're funny now.

I remember such a time with Andy. He was about sixteen and had been saving his money to purchase a special pair of expensive designer jeans. But before I go on with the rest of this story, I need to explain something. We lived in Alabama, the red-clay capital of America. They say the clay is red, but really it's more of a rust color. And when you get it on your clothes, it's almost impossible to get the stain out.

Now that you know that, I can tell you the story. Andy placed his new designer jeans in the clothes hamper. Later that day I was doing a load of laundry when I noticed a pair of jeans covered in red clay stains. The guys usually did their own laundry, but I knew it was going to take some hard work to get the stains out of those jeans.

I worked all morning washing, soaking, and rewashing his jeans, over and over until they were clean.

When he arrived home that afternoon, I proudly presented him with his stain-free jeans. The look on his face was not what I had expected. Instead of a look of gratitude, there was a look of horror. With his kind but sad voice he said, "Oh, Mom, those were the Red Clay jeans I bought with the money I saved."

My heart sank as I began to understand what he was saying. They were Red Clay jeans. They weren't dirty; they were stained by the designer on purpose. *Mommy fail.* Now I can laugh at myself and about my good deed gone wrong, but that night I just wanted to cry.

I would like to tell you that some of the *mommy fails* in your life will someday be turned from tears into laughter. Nobody is perfect! Mom, be encouraged. Your children are not perfect, and neither are you. There is one thing I know I did right: I believed that the Lord could and would do what He had promised.

Believe me, there were many times when I felt like God had given my wonderful boys the wrong mom.

When my children were young, Hank and I attended a banquet to honor the homeschool mom of the year. I listened as they began the introduction of this incredible woman. She had ten children and had homeschooled them all while earning her master's and doctorate degrees. Three of her children were grown—two were doctors and the other was a lawyer. Her family had built their own house. And, oh yes, she'd also taught each child to play a musical instrument! By the time they gave her the award, I just wanted to run out of the room crying because I knew I couldn't do what she had done. I had to remind myself that I only had to homeschool the two children God had given me.

Just remember this: God did not give you the wrong children, and He has not given them the wrong mother. When I felt like I wasn't the right mom for my kids, it was so God could teach me that when I am weak, He is strong. He wants to protect us from becoming puffed up with pride, for as Corrie ten Boom once said, "It is not my ability, but my response to God's ability, that counts."[2] And as God says, "My grace (My favor and loving-kindness and mercy) is enough . . . My strength and power are made perfect (fulfilled and completed) and show themselves most effective in [your] weakness" (2 Corinthians 12:9).

Remind yourself that you don't have to be a supermom, because you have a super God.

TIP 5:

You Can Do Hard Things

I BORROWED THIS PHRASE from my daughter-in-law Mandii. "I can do hard things" is so often her mantra.

Remember, Jesus always calls you to a task that is bigger than your abilities.

That is what happened to me when God gave me children. I'm an only child, and I had never been around babies much, so everything about parenting was new to me. But God did teach me how to be a mom to not only one child but two.

It didn't take long before my husband and I realized that our sons were creative dreamers. Big dreamers. And from the time they were old enough to watch movies, we would hear them talking about becoming filmmakers. We knew very little about the business of creating movies and even less about Hollywood. But we encouraged them and their dreams. And how did we do this?

We encouraged them in conversation. We told them that we hoped and prayed that their dreams would come true and that the result would not only be for their benefit but something that would use the power of this medium to draw people to the Lord Jesus Christ. (Hank's dissertation at seminary, after all, had been "Ministry with Media.")

About this time the Lord led us to pull the boys out of school, and I became a homeschool mom. My education had prepared me to be a teacher in a classroom. This included becoming the principal of a Christian school in Dallas. Yet when Andy was born, I had become a stay-at-home mom. The Lord had quietly said in my heart, *Shelia, set your formal education aside. That is not what I want you to do now.*

Then, when Jon was entering second grade and Andy sixth, God directed me to homeschool our boys. This was not what I had been trained to do. I knew how to run a classroom and even how to run a school—but give up my freedom to stay at home and teach two students? This hadn't been the plan. But long ago I had said yes to Jesus, and if this was my new place, then I would do what He had asked me to do. So day by day I relentlessly and lovingly pursued teaching history, art, mathematics, and economics, all the while embracing the essentials of our faith (I will share some of those essentials with you later).

Once when I told a skeptical gentleman about homeschooling my sons, he condescendingly said, "Lady, you're a dinosaur. What a waste of your education."

A waste of my education? Today, I don't think my sons would agree with that man. In fact, I know they don't agree. Andy has thanked me so many times for being willing to invest in his life. Jon has said that if he had not been homeschooled, he probably would have been a dropout.

As hard as this new path was, I learned more about God's enabling power and that I can do hard things through Him who strengthens me.

TIP 6:

Whose Dream Is It?

As a Christian mom, I desired that my children would follow Christ with their whole hearts, no matter what that looked like. I did not set out to create filmmakers. I just wanted to disciple my children to be personal followers of Jesus.

I often had to remind myself that their dreams were not my calling or dream. It has been amazing to watch God unfold His plan. He put a dream in the hearts of my sons (and it wasn't even the same dream in each of their hearts), and step-by-wonderful-step He led, directed, and fulfilled His plan. It never occurred to me that one day my sons would found a studio dedicated to making Christian movies. My dreams were small. I just believed that someday, in some way, my sons would make a movie. But God knew all along, and He had gone before them and made the path straight.

Moms often say to me, "My child wants to make movies. What did you do to make this happen?" I always laugh a little inside, because it truly has been a God thing, not a mommy thing. This question also makes me a little sad because I hear in it *what* and not *who*. It's a hollow victory when your child finds what the world calls success (money and fame) outside of the will of God. Who my children *are* is so much more important than what they *do*. It thrills me to hear actors and crew members talk about how special my guys make them feel.

At that world premiere of our sons' movie, Hank and I were thrilled that we were seeing their dreams come true. That they were doing what God had called and gifted them to do. All of that would be empty if they were not who God wanted them to be. My answer to this question would not be any different if the *what* were different. Several years ago, Andy said to me, "Mom, you always used to say, 'Find out what God has called you to do, and do it with all your heart.' I used to think that meant I had to be a pastor or a missionary to have a calling, but as I've grown in the Lord, I know that making motion pictures is truly my calling."

The answer to that question—"What did you do to make this happen?"—is always the same: Just follow the Lord with all your heart, give your children encouragement, believe in them, and then trust the Lord with the outcome.

God's plans are so much bigger than our dreams. Max Lucado says it so well: "We're thinking, *Preserve the body*; he's thinking, *Save the soul.* We dream of a pay raise. He dreams of raising the dead. . . . We rejoice at our successes. He rejoices at our confessions. We show our children the Nike star with the million-dollar smile and say, 'Be like Mike.' God points to the crucified carpenter with bloody lips and a torn side and says, 'Be like Christ.'"[1]

I wonder if Billy Graham's mom ever thought that her son would reach the world with the message of salvation through

Christ. You see, my real dream, joy, and delight is not my sons' success but the fact that right now in Russia people who will never darken the door of a church are watching *I Can Only Imagine* in their own language. They are hearing the gospel though a film that my sons gave two years of their lives to make. It was a task that they and their families were willing to make sacrifices for that no one will ever know about, except for Jesus. Their little dreams long ago were infused, filled, and changed into a bigger dream—that of reaching the world with the gospel of Christ through film. Who knows what else God has in store for them?

We have to be careful not to try to live our lives through our children. We don't want to force them to fulfill our dreams. The way to keep this in check is to pray. Pray that your children follow God's plan for their lives—not your plan and not even their plan. The most important thing to remember is that God has a plan for your child's life (see Jeremiah 29:11-13). You do not know what that plan is. His plan is often a progressive plan where He shows us only a little bit at a time. In Psalm 119:105 we are told, "Your word is a lamp to my feet and a light to my path." If you have ever walked in the dark with a flashlight, you can understand this. The flashlight gives us only enough light for the next few steps.

Only God and then your child can know what that dream or plan is. But even if God lets you in on it, your role is praying. Your children's calling is between them and their Lord. I prayed a lot, and you can too.

TIP 7:

They Are Lent to You

EACH TIME HANK AND I DISCOVERED we were expecting a baby, we dedicated the child to the Lord. We understood that God lent our children to us. First Samuel 1:27-28 says, "For this child I prayed, and the Lord has granted my petition made to Him. Therefore I have given him to the Lord; as long as he lives he is given to the Lord."

Even as Abraham in Genesis 22:10 was willing to put his son on the altar before the Lord, we, too, must have the same attitude of trust. I am so thankful that we did this because God tested our willingness to trust Him with Jon.

Thirty-four years ago, I sat in an ambulance, the sound of sirens and speeding cars all around me, with my three-year-old child lying on a stretcher behind me.

It was the end of a busy summer as we were relocating from a church in Ohio back to our home church in Birmingham, Alabama.

Hank and I had left our two boys at their nana's in Gadsden, Alabama, while we went to Birmingham to look for a house.

We spent the day talking to the pastoral staff and getting some leads on houses in the area. Everything seemed to be going great until the phone rang that Wednesday morning. It was my mother. She was calling to inform us that Jonathan was very sick and that they would meet us at the doctor's office in Gadsden, which was about an hour away from us.

When we arrived, my father met us in the parking lot of the doctor's office. Hank stopped to get an update on Jonathan's condition while I ran into the office. They showed me to a back room where my mother was sitting beside Jon, who was lying down experiencing stomach pain.

After the doctor ran some tests, he sent us home with medicine, and we all waited to see if it would heal Jon. At my mother's home, he only continued to get sicker and sicker. It was a long night, as he didn't want me to leave his side.

By morning the doctor decided it was time we leave for the hospital. After many more tests, he walked into our room looking grim and began to share the bad news. He believed that Jon had something wrong with his intestines and didn't offer us a great deal of hope. He wanted us to take him to a hospital in Birmingham, where a Dr. Marshall would perform any necessary surgery.

I rode in the ambulance, feeling helpless and experiencing more grief than I had ever known as I watched my sweet little baby. It was an hour-long drive to the hospital. Anguish to the point of speechlessness is the way to describe how I felt from the time we were given the report. I could only communicate with my heavenly Father. I had been taught to bring every thought captive under the control of our Lord Jesus Christ, and I needed to be comforted and encouraged, so I turned to the Scriptures hidden in my heart for such a day as this. The first passage that came to mind was "When I am afraid, I put my trust in you" (Psalm 56:3, ESV). Then I recalled Romans 8:28: "All things work together for good, for those who are called according to his purpose" (ESV). Not all things *are* good, but they work together *for* our good.

The Lord reminded me that in 1 Samuel 1:27-28, Hannah had given her son to the Lord, and so had I given my Jon to Him. I understood Jon was not mine. He belonged to God. Therefore, God had every right to do with him as He thought best.

I also remembered, as I had been taught in Romans 6, that I had reckoned myself dead. I no longer had any rights; I had been bought with a great price. I no longer belonged to myself but instead to Jesus. The Lord then reminded me that He knew what it was like to see His Son suffer. He actually knew how I felt and even shared my pain.

In James 1, we're told to consider it completely joyful when we are enveloped (and I was enveloped) in trials of any sort. Verse 4 tells us that after the trial performs its perfect work, producing the ability to abide with Christ under pressure, then we will be lacking in nothing. In other words, this was for my good and an opportunity to trust my heavenly Father in a hard place.

A friend also came to my mind that day. Jesus had been her all in all in an even harder place. She had lost her son two years earlier, and she had said to me many times in those years after his death that Jesus *really* is enough. I realized if Jesus had been enough for her, He could be enough to get me through this day. As my spirit began to calm down, I learned I only had to trust Him one minute or second at a time. He knew all about this before the beginning of time. He knew and He could be trusted to do whatever was best. As I continued to draw upon the resources my Father had poured into my life, I began to feel His peace that surpasses all understanding filling my heart and soul.

I was working to actually believe all the things that I'd been taught up until that day, when Abraham came to mind. His son was a miracle child. We almost lost Jonathan, whose name means "gracious," at birth. I went into labor in my sixth month of pregnancy. They were able to get it stopped, but I had to spend the rest of my pregnancy in bed. I did not carry him full-term. Jon was born prematurely and almost died during childbirth, but God had been gracious to give us our own miracle baby. The passage that came to my mind was "After these events, God tested and proved Abraham" (Genesis 22:1).

Like Abraham, I was at the point of a decision. Adversity will either crush or break us. Crushing causes bitterness, but breaking brings about yielding to God. I remembered that our Lord had to make such a decision in the garden of Gethsemane, when He said, "Abba, [which means] Father, everything is possible for You. Take away this cup from Me; yet not what I will, but what You [will]" (Mark 14:36).

As much as I love my two sons, I didn't want to be contrary to God's will. So I proclaimed by faith, "Nevertheless, let Thy will be done this day," even as Job said, "Though he slay me, yet will I trust in him" (Job 13:15, KJV).

So that afternoon I did what Abraham had done with his son. I had already put both of my boys on the Father's altar while they were still in my womb. But that afternoon I had to go one step further: I had to be willing to trust the Lord with the fact that Jon might die.

At that point, I remembered that I had been taught that sickness happens for one of three reasons:

1. unto death
2. for chastisement
3. for the Father's glory

I asked my Father which of these correlated with Jonathan's sickness. *Were these numbered days all that are written in Your book for my son's life?* The Lord gave me peace that it was not so. *Is this for chastisement?* I searched my heart again, and the answer was no.

With those two questions answered, it remained that this must be for the Father's glory. God's peace and love carried me in His arms all the rest of the way to the hospital. Jonathan was still sick, but I knew he would live and that my Father would be glorified.

Doctors ran more tests when we arrived at the hospital. We learned that Jonathan had a ruptured appendix and peritonitis. (Only two out of ten children live with this condition.) Jonathan was prepped for surgery, and when our family gathered in the waiting room, my husband, Hank, led us in prayer. "Father, You know my will and my desire for Jonathan is that he would live, but Father, whatever happens, I will trust You." Hank had followed the ambulance to the hospital in the car behind us and had also been meditating on these two truths: God will give us the desires of our hearts, and "Nevertheless, let Thy will be done." In other words, he had told the Lord that our human hearts' desire was for Jon to live here on earth with us, but we would pray as Jesus prayed in the garden of

Gethsemane ("yet not what I will, but what You [will]") and leave the results to God.

Those were two long weeks of painful recovery, but God gave Jonathan back to us for a second time.

After thirty-four years, the pain in the memory of that day is gone. Was God glorified? It would take another book to tell you all the ways. We learned that the trial of our faith is precious and it produced just what God said it would. It filled up that which was lacking, and we were one step closer to His likeness. He is a faithful, comforting, strengthening, caring, and understanding Savior. He is a man of sorrows acquainted with our grief. What a Savior!

Have you given your children over to God? Maybe you need to do a little soul work right now, before we talk about discipline.

TIP 8:

Discipline Your Children

HOW HAVE WE DISCIPLINED OUR CHILDREN? Often! Seriously, my mother gave me some wonderful advice when I was pregnant with our first child. She said, "Shelia, if you're not going to be consistent with your training and disciplining of this child, then don't do it at all." From that day on, I have sought to be consistent with our children.

In our home, we decided to follow these statements: *We will be faithful to discipline our children. Rebellious and disobedient behavior that does not please the Lord will be quickly and consistently stopped, and discipline will occur.*

Let's define *discipline* (instruction) as "training of mind and character, order among, particular system of rules for conduct, to bring under control, and to chastise or punish." *Instruct* means "to give direction or order to, inform, and to fill up that which is lacking."

All children have an old sin nature! I believe that my job as a parent is to know my children, really know them. That means I must spend a great deal of time with them. I have to find out where they are lacking and what their needs are. I am then supposed to either meet that need or correct them so they are not lacking in that area.

Our heavenly Father is the best example I know of for disciplining His children, so let's look at five ways He disciplines us.

1. *Example*: He calls us to follow His example and to become like Him.

2. *Love*: He loves us just the way we are, and He makes sure we know He loves us. He tells us over and over again that He loves us. He loved us so much that He acted on that love and made sure we would be lacking in nothing.

3. *Instruction*: His law is grace. He gives us instruction about our limitations so that we can be safe. He instructs us on our responsibilities and teaches us to respect others.

4. *Warning*: He tells us the consequences of our sin. He appeals to our conscience. He says, in effect, "If you *do this*, I will *do that*. So please don't."

5. *Correction*: He follows through on His warnings and disciplines His own.

Some of the methods for training children that I've learned over the years are:

- *Instruction by word of mouth or written instruction.* We must make sure our children understand our expectations of them. This means that when they are very young, we must always repeat the rules in our home until they understand them.

- *Learning through observation.* We must be holy examples to our children. Children learn so much through observation.

- *Chastisement or correction.* To disobey always meant chastisement in our home. Hank was so good at correction with our sons. He would always ask them, "Now, what have you learned from this, and how will you do it differently next time?"

Tips on Chastisement

The first thing I always did with my sons when I had to chastise them was to establish personal responsibility. Try to get your child alone and to reflect grief over his or her sin. Please call it sin and not a mistake or making a bad decision. God calls it sin and so should we. Our Father grieves over sin. Ask your child, "What did you do?" Establish God as the final authority. Always associate correction with love.

I will never forget when five-year-old Andy came home from playing with a young friend and asked me why his friend's mother didn't love him. I then asked Andy why he thought this mother didn't love her son. His answer says it all: "Mom, because he's so disobedient, and she does not help him obey. He's going to grow up and sin, and they will put him in jail because she did not love him enough to make him obey."

1. Have a few rules, and make sure they are necessary and that everyone knows what they are.

We established our family purpose: "To know Him and make Him known." Additionally, we set our goal: "We only do that which pleases God." Then we made the rules for our home based on those two things; we didn't require a long list of rules.

2. Be consistent and impartial.

Don't make rules you do not plan on enforcing. If you become inconsistent in parenting, have a family meeting and tell the children that the Lord has convicted you about this and you want them to know you plan on changing. Inconsistency will cause your child to disobey because they know that you will let them get by with bad behavior.

Being impartial is also important in parenting if you have more than one child. Although each of your children is different, make sure the rules and the consequences are the same for all of your children. I have seen the harm it does to a family when one parent has a favorite. Read the life of Joseph in the Bible if you want a picture of what can happen to a family when the parents are not impartial. To stress the idea of being impartial, I once asked each of my children a question.

"Who decides if you are disciplined?" I asked.

"You and Dad do," they each replied.

"No, that's the wrong answer," I said. "Do you know what the rules in our home are? Do you know that Mom and Dad have committed to do what God tells us in the Bible to do, and that God has told us that we must discipline you when you disobey? Do you know that if you disobey, you will be disciplined? Because the answer to all of those questions is yes, who decides if you're disciplined?"

It might take a while, but they will finally come up with the right answer: They are responsible for being disciplined because they chose to disobey.

In fact, I had a funny conversation with Jon when he was five years old. He asked me why he got disciplined so much more than Andy.

"Your brother has discovered a wonderful secret," I said. "Do you want to know what it is?"

"Yes!"

"Andy knows that if he obeys the rules, he won't get disciplined."

Jon looked at me in amazement and said, "I think I could do that!" From that day on he was a different child.

3. Don't argue. Enforce.

4. Don't nag.

After you are sure they understand the rules, telling them once is enough. Telling your child over and over to do the same thing is nagging. Slow obedience is no obedience.

5. Stop the little things.

That way you will have fewer big things to deal with.

6. No sarcasm or ridicule.

Deal with the sin! Call sin what it is: sin.

7. Don't make threats you can't carry out.

8. Make your children take personal responsibility for their sin.

Have them say, "I was wrong to do such and such." Help them name their sin to you, and help them verbalize it back to the

Lord Jesus in prayer. If their sin has hurt anyone, help them seek that person's forgiveness. We did not let them say, "I'm sorry." I thought that statement could mean various things, while the statement "I was wrong to do such and such. Will you forgive me?" could mean only one thing: "I was wrong!"

9. After the discipline is over, reassure them of your love.

Comfort them. Remember, your goal is to get your children's wills under the control of our Lord Jesus Christ. Do not break their spirits. Remember what 1 Timothy 1:5 says about love and instruction: "The object and purpose of our instruction and charge is love, which springs from a pure heart and a good (clear) conscience and sincere (unfeigned) faith."

Our goal was to love our children enough to equip them to respond to God. As 2 Timothy 2:22 says, "Shun youthful lusts . . . aim at and pursue righteousness (. . . conformity to the will of God in thought, word, and deed); [. . . pursue] faith, love, [and] peace." We disciplined our sons in these three areas: thought, word, and deed. Attitudes counted in our home: We didn't allow sitting down on the outside and standing up on the inside. We taught them how they could know God for themselves, and in doing so, they learned to pursue faith, love, and peace. Start early, work hard, walk with the Lord, and be consistent. If you do this, when your children reach the teen years they will give you rest, not trouble.

Discipline is not just the action we take when our children disobey us. It's a consistent walk in our homes. We seek to lead obedient lives as adults. Then our children in turn learn to live that kind of life as well.

What are the goals for your children? What are the rules

in your home, and does everyone understand what they are? It would be helpful for you to sit with your husband to pray and talk about this. Take the goals that the two of you have created and make a list of rules for your home. It's important that you are both in agreement with these and that the children know you are. Perhaps only a few rules are necessary, but make sure each child knows what they are. Sometimes parents get upset with their children about things they do and later find out that the children had no idea that what they were doing was wrong.

I remember when God reminded me to make sure that Jon knew all the rules in our home. With our firstborn, Andy, I spent so much time making sure he knew what we expected of him that I guess I thought Jon would just get it by osmosis.

With Andy, I had put up pegs on the wall and made little denim drawstring bags with a picture painted on the outside of each for each of his toys. The rule was that he had to put his toy back in the right bag before getting another bag down. Andy loved his bags and keeping his room in order.

Then Jon entered the picture! By that time, a friend had made us a large toy box, and the rule was that the toys had to go back in the toy box by bedtime. This was just fine with Andy, and when instructed to clean his room, he did so with great diligence and delight. On the other hand, I saw that Jon really didn't care if the room was neat. I soon learned that because he had ADHD, he could only be told to do one task at a time, such as, "Go pick up all of your G.I. Joe figures, then tell me when you're done." I learned that I had to repeat the rules over and over to him until he got it.

Your children will try to divide and conquer, so you need to have a rule in place to deal with this. We expressed to our children that as their parents, Hank and I were on the same page and that we would support each other's decisions. This is not to say we always agreed, but if we disagreed, we talked about it in private, not in front of the children. Our rule for them was simple: "If one of us tells you no about something and you ask the other parent for a different answer, it's always counted as disobedience, and you will be disciplined." Hank and I tried to remember to ask, "Have you talked to (Mom or Dad) about this?" before we gave an answer.

We wanted our children to learn to obey, but we also wanted to give them a voice, so we set up a way for them to interact with us. If we gave them a command and they did not agree with us, they could sweetly say, "May I speak, please?" We could respond yes or no. If the answer was no, they knew to not say another word and just obey—with joy. If yes was the answer, they were allowed to tell us what was on their heart. As long as they spoke in a respectful tone, they could talk, but if they started to be disrespectful, we would say, "Stop," and then they would have to obey. We never allowed our children to speak to us in a disrespectful way!

Sometimes they would give us information that made us want to change our mind. We would say, "Oh, I didn't know that," and change our instructions. They also knew that our response may be, "That's a great point, but it's irrelevant." At that point, they just had to obey with joy. I have seen my teenage sons bite their lips and walk away as they obeyed without agreeing.

Irrelevant was a word we used early on with our sons. I remember when Andy was three years old, we were walking down the hallway on the way to Sunday school. I don't know what we were talking about, but my answer had been, "Andy, that is irrelevant." A woman stopped me and in a condescending voice said, "That baby does not understand what *irrelevant* means!" I turned to Andy and said, "Son, what does *irrelevant* mean?" He looked at her and in his sweet little-boy voice said, "Not pertaining to the matter." Enough said!

Your children will blunder and engage in childish or immature behavior, but this does not include disobedient behavior. Use this as a time to teach them about responsibility. One such time for us happened when Jon was about five. Hank was watching the boys while I was out shopping. Hank noticed that he could not hear Jon playing in his room anymore. As Hank got up to find him, Jon came in the front door with great joy. He looked up at Hank and said, "Dad, come with me. I have a surprise for you." When Hank walked out the door, he could see that Jon had been busy washing his car. Jon looked up at him and said, "Dad, how do you like it?" Hank told him that it was the best job he had ever seen a five-year-old do. Then he added, "Next time you might want to roll up the window before you start." Jon said, "You know, Dad, that's a great idea."

If your children break something in their childishness, they will need to replace it. Make them work to earn the money to do this.

As you begin this process of training your children through discipline, you're going to have to take an honest look at who they really are. Sometimes this is hard and even scary, but you have to be honest with yourself about them if you're going to be able to help them become all that God wants them to be. You have to be willing to believe and see that your child has weaknesses, faults, and flaws that need correcting.

We are to teach, train, and make disciples of our children, but what does that look like? Once there was a mom who had been meeting with me for several weeks. She wanted some help with parenting her three children, one older child and her eighteen-month-old twins. She called me to say she might have to cancel because her friend could only babysit two of the children. I encouraged her to come anyway. I thought this might be a good time to practice some of what I had been teaching her.

She arrived at my house with one of her eighteen-month-olds. We went into the living room to sit on the floor when she looked at me in horror. She remembered my glass-house collection was on the bottom shelf of one of the living room tables. I assured her everything in my house belonged to the Lord, not me, and that this would be a great time to train her child.

We sat down on the floor, her with her child in her lap. The child quickly spotted the houses and crawled over to them. I instructed this mom to look at her child and say no. Then, when that didn't work, I instructed her to say no again, spank the child's hand, and say no again in a stern voice. She did, but the child kept touching the houses. I instructed her to do it again, but this time to spank the child's hand and put her back on her lap. She then started to do something I am sure we have all done—she reached in her bag to get a toy. I said, "Not yet."

The child started back over to the houses. I told her to repeat the process. We did this several times; then I said, "Now take the toy out and put it parallel to the houses, and with your sweetest, happiest voice while touching the toy say, 'Yes, yes.' Afterward, look back at the houses and say, 'No, no.'" It only took two more times for the child to choose the toy. We clapped, and so did she! I instructed the mother to give her daughter several more toys to play with while we talked.

When I was still in college, Hank and I were friends with one of the professors and his wife. All of us, including their toddler daughter, went to one of Hank's baseball games. When we got to the field, the mother used a stick to draw a line in the dirt. She then looked at her child and said, "No, no, do not cross over this line." She gave her daughter some toys to play with and sat down in her chair. I remember thinking, *Right, that child will never stay behind that line.* To my amazement she did just that. Several times she went over to the line and put her foot on the line and looked back at her mom as if to ask if it was still a no. The mom would just shake her head and say, "No, no." I was in awe! It was clear to me that that the mom had done some major training with her at home.

Make sure you are training them for the outcome you really want. I was on the phone with a young mom when her child came in the room to ask to go out on the front porch. The mother said, "No, your dad is on the phone, and he does not need to be interrupted." Good so far, right? She continued to allow the child to ask questions, four of them, about going out on the porch. After the child left the room and because I had been invited to be a part of helping her learn better ways to deal with her children, I said, "You did that all wrong."

She asked, "What should I have done?" We had been working on hand signals. So I told her, "When you are on the phone or talking with a friend in person, your child is to touch your arm. You are to then hold your hand up in a stop gesture so they know that they have your attention. You then say to your friend, 'Excuse me, but my child needs something.' You then turn and ask them what they need. When they tell you what they need, you give them an answer *one time*, and they are to obey. If they do not obey, you then tell your friend that you will call her back. Then you stop to discipline your child for disobedience. When your child does it right, make sure you tell her how proud you are of her and maybe give her a reward when you get off the phone."

Training is hard work but well worth it. It's much easier just to pacify your children than to do the work of training. But believe me, it's easier to train a two-year-old than to deal with a rebellious sixteen-year-old.

Remember, the purpose for discipline is love that springs from a pure heart. Children spell *love* differently than we do. They spell *love* T-I-M-E. We live in a hurry, hurry, and hurry world. We have to stop and spend time with our children. Believe me, you will turn around twice and they will have children of their own.

I have heard it said that there are these distinct stages of parenting:

- Birth to five years: when you discipline and hopefully bring them to Christ
- Six to twelve years: when you teach them and train them to walk in the Spirit
- Thirteen to nineteen years: when you coach them, because you can't play the game for them
- Twenty years and up: when you counsel, befriend, and consult

I was starting the coaching stage with my sons when I asked some of the young basketball players at our church what they thought made a good coach. They listed loving the game, understanding the game, wanting to win, and motivating the team to win. They also said a good coach must discipline players to get better.

A childhood friend of mine, John Coyle, said, "When our children are born, we are given a suitcase, and we have about eighteen years to pack it for life."

I remember like yesterday when we packed our firstborn son's suitcase for him to attend Bible school in New York. I remember wondering as we packed that suitcase if his life suitcase was packed well. Dear moms, you are equipping a human being to be used by God, a disciple, so pack well. You may want to sit down and make a list of ten or fifteen things that you want to make sure you pack in your child's suitcase for life.

At the time of writing this, my sons are now in their thirties and forties and have children of their own. Just the other day I was discussing parenting with Jon, and I told him that I have increasingly seen that the character traits—aspects of behavior intertwined with personality—that I had to discipline him and Andy for because of their childish lack of control, and the ones that drove me crazy, are the very character traits that God is using in their adult lives to accomplish His will, under the control of the Holy Spirit. You may be asking yourself why your child is a certain way. But the correct perspective might be to thank God for the way He has made that child and ask how you can help equip this person to be best used by God.

As Paul stated in 2 Corinthians 12:10 (emphasis added), "For *when I am weak* [in human strength], then *am I* [truly] *strong* (able, powerful in divine strength)." In other words, Jesus can take those weaknesses and turn them into great strengths. My dear parent, take courage. Instead of asking why God made a child the way He did in a negative way, ask the Lord, *What do You have for this child?*

TIP 9:

God Enables You

GOD ENABLES US TO DO what He's called us to do, and this is also true for your children and their God-given dreams.

Our sons' journey into filmmaking started long before Andy and Jon were born. It began with Hank's love for radio and television. Hank worked at KCBI radio in Dallas to help pay for seminary. After a year at KCBI, the news director of Channel 11 TV asked Hank to join their team. Our sons grew up thinking all daddies were on TV. In fact, when Andy was three, he watched his dad do the evening news each night at 6 p.m. One night I was cooking dinner and I stepped into the den to see a story Hank was doing, and while I was watching it, a grease fire started on the stove. I put a lid on the pan to put it out. Andy ran back into the den and held his hand out to the TV set and said, "It's okay, Dad, Mom put the fire out." He thought his dad could hear him!

Later on, when Hank was doing a live local cable TV show each night, Andy and Jon, then sixteen and twelve, were allowed to work on their dad's set. They loved working with cameras, and soon they began to help out around the station, working in the booth and assisting with other shows. They caught the bug, and God began to train them for their calling.

They began to work for the same station as cameramen for high-school football games. They learned how to edit and work all the machines in the sound and production booth. Being homeschooled, they had a flexible schedule that allowed for this.

About that time, they decided to start a business being photographers. A dear friend had given them a nice camera, and they had taken a class (from Jon's now father-in-law!). They decided they would take photos for schools' sporting events. That first entrepreneurial effort lost money, but it was a great learning experience. They learned that not all dreams succeed.

Not long after that is when our guys came to their dad and announced, "We think God wants us to make movies someday." That night Hank did not discourage them; in fact, he encouraged them to dream big. He told them that God could do anything, and he told them two things that would make the difference in everything they tried to do. The first was what he called "the wow factor": If someone sees your work and says, "That's nice," you're not done. You go back and work some more until they say, "Wow!"

He also told them it would take twenty years for them to be successful filmmakers. He told them something that he truly believed with all his heart: God is a miracle worker, and if you follow Him, there's no limit to what you can do. Andy and Jon went into their room, got down on their knees, and asked God to make them film directors. That night, Erwin Brothers

Entertainment was born. (Mom, never forget that God has a plan for your creative dreamers and that what He calls them to do He will enable them to do as they follow Him with their whole hearts.) So, given that what God called our sons to do He enabled them to do, God began the process of training them to do their calling.

After graduating from high school, Andy attended Word of Life (WOL) Bible Institute in New York. That summer Andy was put in charge of making videos of the campers at WOL summer camp, videos for the campers to take home at the end of each week. He called us to ask if Jon could work with him that first summer. After much prayer, fourteen-year-old Jon went to work for his big brother.

That first venture into filmmaking was successful, although Jon said the first video they made was a lesson for him. He thought the video was great. He sat in the audience to hear the campers' response to it, and the boy next to him said, "Is that it?" He said he never wanted to hear that again (in fact, on movie premiere nights, you'll find Jon pacing in the lobby). The boys took their dad's advice about the wow factor, and the camp went from losing money to making a great deal of money from the sale of those videos. The best part was that the gospel was in each and every video that the campers took home with them. Parents would watch them and hear about Jesus.

That summer the name for their company was born. At Word of Life, they soon became known as the Erwin Brothers.

For the next two summers Jon joined his brother at the WOL camps. This began the next part of God training them to be filmmakers. They learned how to please an audience as well as new techniques of filmmaking, but most of all they learned that God could take a few resources and do much with them. The two of them had very little equipment, and they would have many all-nighters working to produce those videos at WOL. I remember one summer being at camp with some of our teens from Alabama and seeing the boys improvising to make the equipment work. Step-by-step, God was beginning to answer their prayer.

Mike Falgout, a young man from our church who did free-lance camera work, had worked with Hank on several projects. The boys learned a lot from Mike over the years, and Jon began to intern for Mike. He was a godsend, helping Jon learn so much about being a cameraman. This eventually led to Jon working a camera for ABC at the age of fifteen, which then led to him working with ESPN filming college football.

With Andy off at school, Jon made his bedroom into a film studio. Hank helped him get his first camera and his first editing computer. With this he started making videos for churches and missionaries to help them tell their stories in order to raise money for the mission field. Again, Jon took his dad's advice about the wow factor, and the business began to grow without even advertising. Jon even had one intern, a fellow home-schooler, who came to our house three afternoons a week to work with Jon. This young man worked with the guys for a long time until he became a freelance cameraman for ESPN.

In the meantime, because of the work that he had done for WOL, Andy was asked by the management there to work full-time for the Bible school as their videographer.

Jon's video business had grown so much that it was more work than he could handle. Hank asked me, "What do you think about Andy coming home and working with Jon?"

"As long as he knows it's okay with us if he stays at Word of Life if that's what God has for him," I answered.

Hank called Andy that morning to ask him what he thought about working with Jon. Andy told his dad that his timing was unbelievable, because he was supposed to sign his contract with WOL that day. He told his dad that he was going to ask for advice from some of the men on staff at the school. Later that day Andy called to tell us that everyone he talked to asked him the same thing. The question was, "Is working at Word of Life your dream?" His answer was always the same: "No, my dream is to make movies someday with my brother." They told him to go home and follow his dream. He told us that day that he was coming home.

Jon told Andy that he was working on the weekends for a new company by the name of ESPN and that Andy could free-lance with them as well. (For many years, they worked on the weekends for ESPN and during the week for Erwin Brothers. Working as camera operators for football games soon became their full-time career. They eventually worked on everything from ESPN College Football Primetime to Fox NFL doing events such as the X Games and the Super Bowl. In those years, they didn't take a salary from the Erwin Brothers business. Jon said it was their hobby gone wild.) They worked together that year until Jon graduated from high school. Andy told Jon that he wanted him to have the college experience for at least one year. We had also told our boys that no matter what they wanted to do with their lives, we wanted them to attend one year of Bible school. So off to WOL Jon went, while Andy stayed in Alabama and ran the Erwin Brothers business.

The next year when Jon returned from school, business had

grown to the point that they needed an office. At that time, the boys' business filmed missionary videos, weddings, and commercials. The back office of our ministry in Alabaster, Alabama, wasn't being used, so they rented that from us. They stayed there for several years, taking up more and more space until all we had was an office at the front, which was fine, because by this time Hank was serving his first term as a state senator.

Jon and Andy began to look for office space and found a building for sale not far from our office. They asked us what we thought. It looked like they had done their homework and it was a good investment. Everything was in place; the financing had been secured and they were ready to go.

Then I was in Bible study one morning when the Lord said to me, "Shelia, this is not the way that I've worked with your sons. That office is not what I have for them."

I was dreading having to tell my sons what God said to me, when Jon made a comment about the building not being a long-term answer for them, and at that point, I asked them if I could talk to them. I told them what God had said and asked them if they would be willing to hold off on buying the office so they could see what God would do. They said, "Sure, no problem."

Jon had received a phone message a few weeks earlier from someone he didn't know. This person contacted him again. The call was about an office large enough for a studio. The owners would build the inside for Andy and Jon just the way they wanted it and rent it to them for five years. It was an incredible space and was so much better than the other facility. My sons began to design the office and studio, and several months later they moved in. Through this they learned to wait on God and that His plan was always better than theirs.

Also, step-by-step, God began to teach them how to make a movie. He did this by giving them a project that was just a little bit outside their skill sets. As they were faithful to learn new skills, He would give them another assignment.

Remember, Mom, just as God was faithful to enable our sons to do what He had called them to do, He will do the same for your children as well. Second Chronicles 16:9 says, "For the eyes of the Lord run to and fro throughout the whole earth to show Himself strong in behalf of those whose hearts are blameless toward Him."

Join in the Fun and Be Their Fan

As God enables your children to grow their skills on the way to fulfilling their callings, you may have a chance to come alongside them. And you can certainly be their biggest fan! Here's how our sons progressed in their callings and how we were able to join in their fun.

Andy and Jon's first step into the world of film came when a company they'd filmed commercials for asked them to do a twenty-five-minute short film on Patrick Henry's speech where he famously said, "Give me liberty or give me death." So, with a budget of $25,000, they began the process of making *The Spirit of Liberty*.

In those days, it was a family project to make their films. Jon called me, using his famous Mom-I-need-something voice. "Mom, could you and Connie make some coats for us?" (Jon had married by this time, and Connie was his mother-in-law and my dear friend).

"I think we can," I said. "How many do you need?"

"Oh, about seventy."

"What!" I said. "How long do we have to make them?"

"Two weeks."

Connie was and is the head of one of the largest home-school groups in Alabama, so we set up shop at the school headquarters. We bought all the cheap fabric we could find, and for the next two weeks homeschool moms came to our aid. Some of the moms could not sew, but they could cut patterns. Some took the coats home to work on them. When Andy and Jon were ready to film, we were gluing buttons on—but we got it done.

When the filming began, the homeschool community pro-vided extras and help of all kinds. It turned out to be a good video. So began the teamwork process and Jon's favorite quote, "If you see a turtle on a fence post, you can be sure he had some help getting up there."

Then they began to venture into making documentaries and short films written by Jon, directed by Erwin Brothers Entertainment, and edited by Andy.

In 2009, Jon and Andy produced and directed their multi-award-winning documentary about a 9/11 story, *The Cross and the Towers*. It was their first film project to air on national TV, and we all met at their office to watch it together for a night to remember. It still airs on national TV on 9/11 each year.

Another change in direction came when Michael W. Smith asked them to do a music video for his song "How to Say Goodbye." This began their adventure into filming Christian music videos.

The Christian music group Casting Crowns asked them to film the video for their song "Slow Fade." As the planning for this production began, Jon called me again with his famous

Mom-I-need-something voice. He remembered that I had taught a class on making faux stained-glass windows, so he told me that day that he needed two faux stained-glass windows for the video. He asked if Connie and I could help him out. I never learn, so I said, "Sure. How big do they need to be?"

"Three feet by seven feet" was his reply.

"What?" I said with a laugh.

I spent the night designing the two large windows. Connie gathered about ten women to help with the project. This included Jon's wife, Beth; Andy's wife, Mandii; and Mandii's mom.

Beth and Connie were on their way to the studio to work on this project when Connie said, "Maybe we can use these windows at church on the stage for Easter."

Connie was more than a bit surprised when Beth said, "Oh, Mom, Jon and Andy are going to break them during the filming."

Jon and Andy found their greatest success yet in the world of music, directing music videos and producing concerts and television programs for platinum artists including Amy Grant, Michael W. Smith, Casting Crowns, Switchfoot, Skillet, Montgomery Gentry, and many others. They were honored with wins for Music Video of the Year at the GMA Dove Awards for three years consecutively, as well as receiving a total of eleven nominations. Through this work, they began to learn how to tell visual stories.

The budgets and crew of Erwin Brothers Entertainment are now very large, and we just show up on the set to watch. But to tell the truth, I miss those days of small beginnings when we joined in the fun.

Hank and I moved from being project participants to our sons' fans when we went to the GMA Dove Awards in Nashville the first year they were nominated for Music Video of the Year. We sat in the balcony so we could watch our sons and their wives below. It seemed as if they would never get to their category, and it turned out to be the last award of the night. We were both nervous wrecks. As the presenters read the nominations and showed a clip of each one, we held each other's hands so tight that we almost cut off the circulation. Then they said, "And the winner is 'Slow Fade,' Casting Crowns, filmed by the Erwin Brothers." We jumped up, screaming, laughing, crying, and kissing. Later on that night when we were standing in line to be seated for dinner, the couple in front of us turned around and said, "You must be the parents!" We laughed. I'm sure the guys were glad we were in the balcony! Those early years were hard, but they were also so much fun.

Andy and Jon received their next break when Crown Financial Ministries asked them to direct the international dramatic short film series *God Provides*, where they created a series of 5 fifteen-minute videos teaching lessons about God's provision. Dean Jones agreed to play the part of Abraham, and at the San Antonio Film Festival—where their series was featured, along with Dean Jones being given a lifetime-achievement award—I thanked Dean for doing this for our sons. I'll never forget his response. He said, "Your sons are very gifted moviemakers. They know what they want, and they know how to get that from their actors. I loved working with them." This dear man loved the Lord and was such an encouragement to Andy and Jon over the years until his passing in 2015.

At that film festival Jon met and became friends with Stephen

Kendrick, which led Jon to working with the Kendrick Brothers as second-unit director for their movie *Courageous*. During the filming of that movie, actor Alex Kendrick asked Jon a question that would change the Erwin Brothers' direction forever. Alex asked, "Jon, what's the purpose for your work?" Up until that time, Andy and Jon had been telling other people's stories. They had been, as Jon put it, "the Han Solos" of the film industry.

"I've got a ship," he would say. "And if you need to go somewhere—I'll take you there."

At the same time Jon began to pray about this question, he and Andy had created a video for a pregnancy center in Birmingham. They were invited to attend the banquet where the video would be shown, and the speaker that day was a young woman who had survived a failed abortion when she was a baby. Jon said he never knew that those two words, *abortion* and *survivor*, could go together. As Jon listened to this woman tell her story, God gave him the idea for the script of *October Baby*.

Jon went to work that night and the next morning laid the script on Andy's desk.

"Read this and tell me what you think," he said.

After Andy read the script, he told Jon, "We have to do this."

With the help of Theresa Preston, an Erwin Brothers staff member's wife, the *October Baby* script was finished.

In 2010, with the script in hand, Jon and Andy shifted their focus and stepped into the world of dramatic feature films. The first thing to be done was to raise money to produce this film. The first one-third came from my mother. And once they had the budget of $800,000 in hand, production began.

You may or may not be able to be a part of the fun in your children's work, but you can always be their biggest fan. Here's a little advice: We always waited to be asked into our sons' world of filmmaking, and when they outgrew our ability to help, we stepped aside. You may just be able to stand on the sidelines and cheer them on. I once heard a famous actor thank his mom for her encouragement. She thought everything he did deserved an Academy Award.

TIP 11:

Teach about Disappointment

IS GOD'S PLAN WITHOUT HEARTACHE, hardship, failure, and disappointment? No, but He has promised us that He will never leave us alone. When our children were very young, we began to teach them to bow the knee to the will of God as they watched us do the same. We taught them that God has a plan and that even if it is different from our plan, we will submit to it even if it is painful to do so and thank Him in the midst of it. God can be trusted to direct us both by giving us what we want and by withholding something from us. We taught them that we can even learn from our own failure of not meeting a desired objective. Life is ever teaching us to trust God more and that He is always with us, no matter what.

We have to be careful not to look for a magic bullet. Hank has often told couples who come to us to help them make a decision about a life choice that "there are no perfect choices." What does that mean? When we have reached a conclusion after much prayer and consideration, we should not think that the path we have chosen will be without problems. Actually, the opposite is often the case. But some people believe that if we follow the will of the Father, everything will be smooth sailing.

When Jon was about four years old, he was fishing at my parents' with Andy, who was quite the fisherman. Jon had been fishing before, but he was not very good at it. Because he had ADHD, he never left the hook in the water long enough to catch a fish.

On this day, he had just put his hook in the water, when to his delight, he discovered he had caught a fish. As we were taking the fish off the hook, he looked up at me with those sky-blue eyes and said, "Thank You, Lord!" He continued to fish and hooked another one, but before he could get this one up on the deck, it got away. I never will forget what happened next. Jon again looked up at me and said, "Thank You, Lord. Mom, is that the way to do it?" That day he had learned to give thanks in all things, whether he caught a fish or not.

We have a friend who says that "thank you" is the language of submission and trust. We are saying, "You are God and I'm not; I know that You have promised to make everything work out for Your glory and my good. I will trust You, and I will submit to Your will!"

We all want the blessings of God. We want to see miracles, but we don't want to be in a place where an act of God is the only answer.

Joseph is one of my favorite characters in the Old Testament. I love that seventeen-year-old boy who lived his life to the glory of God. Joseph's life was not easy. He went through much pain and disappointment, giving him every human right to be bitter, angry, and vengeful. However, he chose to trust in God through every circumstance. He learned the wonderful truth that God was with him through all experiences. I have taught his life story many times, and the theme for those studies is that faith is life without scheming. In one particular study, we made magnets for our refrigerators to remind us not to scheme but to trust God when we're disappointed. It's tough to do, I know, because we mothers are wired to fix things. Yet Joseph was not trusting in the people or circumstances of his life to make his life work; he was trusting in his God.

Learning to have faith is not an easy task, but Joseph shows us that it can be done. He believed that even though others may have meant things for evil, God meant them for good. Romans 8:28 says, "And we know that all things work together for good to them that love God, to them who are the called according to his purpose" (KJV). Joseph believed that God does everything for our good and for His glory. Psalm 50:15 instructs us to "call upon me in the day of trouble: I will deliver thee, and thou shalt glorify me" (KJV).

This has been explained to me this way: Imagine I invited you to my house for afternoon tea. Before you arrive, I put my best tablecloth on the table and then go to my garden, cut some roses, and put them in my best vase. Suppose I unpacked my lovely china teapot and cups to use for our tea party and then got out five bowls. I filled one with flour, one with three raw eggs, one with sugar, one with oil, and the last one with milk. When you arrive and we sit down, I ask you as I point to the bowls, "Would you like some cake?" I think as you looked at the bowls you would be sure I had lost my mind. None of those things look like a cake.

But what if, before you came, I took the contents of the bowls, measured out just the right amounts from each bowl, stirred them all together, put them in a cake pan, and baked the combined ingredients? We would have cake for our tea party.

This is just what God promises to do with all those bad things in our life. He makes them work together for good. Joseph believed that, and then he got to live that out in his life.

Teaching your children about Joseph's story and disappointment will help them as they experience the ups and downs of following their callings. When Joseph was only seventeen years old, he had been told by God that he would rule over his father and brothers. But before that happened, he walked through a lot of hard disappointments. He was put in a pit and then sold into slavery by his brothers, who hated him. Then he found great success in Potiphar's house, only to be tempted by his wife, and even though Joseph did the right thing, he was thrown into jail because she lied about him to her husband. Not until he was thirty years old would God's purpose for his life be fulfilled. Through all these obstacles God was ever with Joseph and preparing him to rule. Joseph even told his brothers later that what they had done to him they had meant for evil but God meant for good. Through it all, Joseph had learned that God would never leave him and that God would fulfill His promises. It was God he learned to trust, not circumstances or people, not even his own abilities.

My sons encountered a major obstacle and disappointment with their first feature film. Everything was going great. The movie was finished. Then came the low point. They were told that because of the subject matter no one wanted to distribute the movie in theaters. Even though promises had been made, they were told to just put it out on DVD and try to make their money back.

With this heartbreaking news Andy and Jon went to the Lord in prayer. Had they misheard Him? Would this movie never be shown in theaters? What were they to do? They decided that the Lord wanted this movie to be in theaters. While Andy was editing the movie, Jon set out to raise the $2 million needed to market and distribute the film in theaters.

In the weeks that followed, God tested them. One of my daughters-in-law came to me with a prayer request. (Whenever they come to me with a need, I always ask if they need my help or prayer. This request was for prayer.) She said, "We only have seventy-five cents in our checking account." So we prayed. The next morning, the money Jon had raised began to arrive. But God took them to the end of their human resources before He began to provide.

Samuel Goldwyn Films and Provident Films eventually released their debut feature film, *October Baby*. It opened nationwide in 2012, breaking into the top ten movies showing that first weekend, according to the website Box Office Mojo, while playing on just 390 screens.

Jon and Andy had begun to pray about what would be next when actor/writer/producer/director Kevin Downes came to them with an idea for a comedy called *Moms' Night Out*. Sony Pictures would pay for production and release. Jon began to write the screenplay, and just like that, they stepped into the world of comedy. *Moms' Night Out* is an endearing true-to-life family film that celebrates the beautiful mess called parenting. It, too, ended up in the top ten of box office revenue when it opened, according to Box Office Mojo.

Their third movie would spawn from a bedtime story told to them many times by their father. It was a true story of our lives in the seventies. Sean Astin played Hank in this movie, *Woodlawn*. It's the story of a gifted high-school football player who must learn to boldly embrace his talent and his faith as he battles racial tensions on and off the field. *Woodlawn* is a moving and inspirational film based on the true story of how the love of Jesus overcame hate and division in the early 1970s in Birmingham, Alabama. Again, this movie was in the top ten of box office revenue the weekend it opened, according to Box Office Mojo. As a result of this movie, there were more than twenty-five thousand recorded decisions for Christ. My sons began to see the power of telling a true story.

Mom, start early in the life of your dreamers to teach them how to face disappointments, because they are bound to face difficult obstacles on the way to their dreams and goals. They will need to keep turning to God and trusting His guidance. He will use all of this to train, redirect, and mature them. He may even use failure to transform their dreams into His dream. You never know what God has planned!

TIP 12:

Make Daily Deposits

OUR FIRST NIGHT ON THE SET of *Woodlawn*, I stood in amazement. There were more than two hundred crew members working that night. Family and friends were no longer needed to work the event, but we did get to host all the investors, pastors, and heads of many ministries who had come to watch. While I stood watching my sons run the show, I asked my Lord, *How did we get here?* We got there step by faithful step. I like to call them daily deposits. As moms, we have the joy of building character in our child little by little, moment by moment, day by day. We must make daily deposits in their lives early on; we can't wait until they are teenagers and then decide to start training them for life.

That night, I remembered the first set my sons built. When Andy was six and Jon was two, our church sent us to Ohio to help start a church. That Christmas there was not a lot of money to invest in toys.

As was our yearly custom, we put a moratorium on buying any new toys after the first day of October. The main reason for this was that I had to start early to find bargains to stretch the money I had earned by participating in a craft fair each year for my Christmas budget.

Hank had the joy of introducing the guys to the *Star Wars* movies. They had been able to buy several of the action figures but not any of the ships.

One October afternoon as I was shopping, I came across the find of the year. The store had all of its *Star Wars* toys on sale for 85 percent off. I was able to buy two X-Wing Starfighters, two Millennium Falcons, two Ewok villages, and two All Terrain Armored Transports (AT-AT walkers). I also got many of the action figures they didn't have, including Han Solo, Chewbacca, Luke Skywalker, C-3PO, and R2-D2. What a Christmas morning that was!

The rest of the story happened a year later when our church in Birmingham asked Hank to return home to fill a staff position. We had a large unused space in our garage, so I had a fun idea. What if the boys and I built a *Star Wars* set?

I bought two large pieces of plywood and lots of plaster of paris.

We worked on constructing the set for weeks. The Ewok village was surrounded by the dense forest we had crafted, and we built landing pads for all the spacecraft as well as a Rebel Alliance base camp.

Andy and Jon spent many hours making up stories and playing in our garage with the set we had created.

When I asked Andy, "Can you tell me what was so special about the *Star Wars* set and the Ewok village we built?" his answer blew me away. He said, "It was you entering into my world and helping me tell a story. It was magic. It really sparked imagination. It took a lot of time and care to create. For me, that was one of the first seeds of storytelling that was planted in my development. In that I found my life's calling as a storyteller."

You entered into my world. What a lesson to be learned. So often we moms don't take the time to learn about our children's worlds, much less to enter into those worlds with them. Mom, stop and take time to get to know your dreamer, and then dream with your child. I'm sure my household duties fell by the way-side those hours and days we worked on that set together, but what a memory we made. That memory still warms my heart. Who knows? Maybe it was one of the seeds that God used to steer my boys toward His dream for them. That set was all part of the "daily deposit" process.

The next film that God would give them was the inspirational drama *I Can Only Imagine*, which tells the true story behind the hit Christian song of the same name, written by Bart Millard.

By this time our family had really grown. Andy and Mandii had two children, and Jon and Beth had three. Plans were in place to start filming in Oklahoma City in late October when we learned that Andy and Mandii were expecting a new arrival in September, and Jon and Beth would have an addition to their family four weeks later! What to do? Part of the answer was for Mandii to stay home after the baby was born. This meant Hank and I would stay behind to help her, and Andy would return home on the weekends when he could.

We did get to be on set for the last week of filming. When we arrived in Oklahoma City, the weather was wonderful for December. We didn't even need to wear a coat, but by the end of the week they were forecasting an ice storm, which was a major problem. The final scene, which required more than 2,500 extras, was supposed to be filmed that night. We prayed and moved forward, not knowing if anyone would brave the weather to be an extra and fill the seats in the auditorium.

They filmed all afternoon, then took a dinner break. We all went backstage and waited. One of my sons looked at me and said, "Well, it's time. Let's go see if anybody is out there." He pulled back the curtain, and to our great joy, over half of the seats were full and people were still pouring in. They had to turn people away!

That was a wrap, so Andy began the editing process. Jon and the rest of the team started the publicity campaign. Release of the film was to be March 16, or "3/16," which wasn't planned because of the famous Scripture John 3:16. Jon hadn't even thought about it until someone pointed it out to him. For the rest of the time leading up to 3/16, he would say, "I'm Jon, and our movie opens on 3/16. That's right, *Jon 3/16*."

Opening week for the movie started with a gala screening in Nashville, followed by a premiere in Oklahoma City, and ending with the premiere night in Dallas.

On March 16, 2018, we all gathered in Dallas for a party as we waited for the numbers to come in for *I Can Only Imagine*.

Remember what Hank told them? "It will take twenty years for you to become successful filmmakers." He told them something that he truly believed with all his heart—that God is a miracle worker, and if you follow Him, there's no limit to what you can do.

Remember, what God calls us to do He enables us to do.

Guess what? That year marked twenty years since God had begun training them in their callings.

They had not reached that point overnight. There had been years of daily deposits. As moms, we sure enjoy those worth-it moments, but they do not happen unless we are willing to invest thousands of daily deposits in our dreamers' lives. Before they ever made their first movie, Andy and Jon would often ask me, "Mom, do you really think we'll ever make a movie?" I always said the same thing, "Yes, I do!" Every time I answered that question, I was building their confidence and making a deposit into their dream.

Teach Them to Value Others

MOM, JUST A LITTLE WARNING HERE: The success of your dreamer is not due to a one-woman show. You are just one of the people God will use in your dreamer's life. You need to go into this mommy thing with an open hand. I would encourage you to pray that God would prepare other people to speak into your dreamer's life as well.

I shared a passage about the building of the Tabernacle from Exodus with my sons when they were young teens. I don't know if they remember it, but it was a sweet reminder to me of the fact that what God calls us to do He enables us to do, and also that God prepares other people with various gifts to work together so that certain jobs are accomplished.

> And Moses said to the Israelites, See, the Lord called
> by name Bezalel son of Uri, the son of Hur, of the
> tribe of Judah; and He has filled him with the Spirit
> of God, with ability and wisdom, with intelligence
> and understanding, and with knowledge and all

craftsmanship, To devise artistic designs. . . . And God has put in Bezalel's heart that he may teach, both he and Aholiab son of Ahisamach, of the tribe of Dan. He has filled them with wisdom of heart and ability to do all manner of craftsmanship. . . . Bezalel and Aholiab and every wisehearted man in whom the Lord has put wisdom and understanding to know how to do all the work for the service of the sanctuary shall work according to all that the Lord has commanded. . . . And Moses called Bezalel and Aholiab and every able and wisehearted man in whose mind the Lord had put wisdom and ability, everyone whose heart stirred him up to come to do the work; and they received from Moses all the freewill offerings which the Israelites had brought for doing the work of the sanctuary, to prepare it for service. And they continued to bring him freewill offerings every morning. And all the wise and able men who were doing the work on the sanctuary came . . . and they said to Moses, The people bring much more than enough for doing the work which the Lord commanded to do.

EXODUS 35:30-32, 34-36; 36:1-5

What can we learn from this passage? And what can you teach your children about their calling and the value of other workers in God's Kingdom from this Scripture? Several things come to mind:

1. The Lord called them by name. (God knows you and has a plan for your life.)

2. God filled them with His Spirit. (It's God's work, not yours; therefore it requires His power to do it.)

3. God filled Bezalel "with ability and wisdom, with intelligence and understanding, and with knowledge and all craftsmanship, to devise artistic designs" (Exodus 35:31-32). (He has given gifts to us to do the work He has called us to do.)

4. There were others God had prepared to work with them, people who had the ability to do all manner of craftsmanship: "and every able and wisehearted man in whose mind the Lord had put wisdom and ability, everyone whose heart stirred him up to come to do the work" (Exodus 36:2). (Look for these people and bring them into the dream.)

5. Others gave so the work could be done: "freewill offerings which the Israelites had brought for doing the work of the sanctuary, to prepare it for service. And they continued to bring him freewill offerings every morning" (Exodus 36:3). (Pray that God will bring others to give so the work can be done.)

6. The people brought much more than enough for doing the work that the Lord commanded them to do. (He can and will provide for the work He has called us to do.)

While watching the installation of a new bathtub in our home, I learned a lot about this Exodus passage and how the body of Christ is supposed to work! Watching those men work was like watching a waltz. There were many things that had to be done to install my new tub, and each step required an expert. First the carpenter came to build the frame, and then the plumbers placed the tub in just the right place and connected all the pipes. After that, the electricians connected the jets, the carpenter finished his work, the stonecutter made a beautiful shelf around the tub, the Sheetrock guys did their work, and then the painters finished things off. When they were done, my new tub looked like it had always been there. This was all done like clockwork because each person did what they were trained to do. No one tried to do it all. They respected the other person's work. There was a contractor who managed the project and told each person when to come and what needed to be done.

I have seen this concept at work in many places, but none so real as the work that my sons have had the privilege of being the contractors for. There were others He had prepared to work with them. There have been so many people in the body of Christ who have been at just the right place, at just the right time, with just the right skill set and with just the right heart for the Lord to do unbelievable things. They have come alongside to help protect, encourage, direct, and provide for my sons.

What Hank and I started they have continued to do. Mom, pray that God will do this for your dreamers as well. They will need others in the body of Christ to fulfill their God-given dreams. Every person's gift is important. God wants us to be a symphony, not just soloists.

My sons also had help with the making of *I Can Only Imagine*, which ended up being a huge success that made more than $83 million in the domestic box office. None of us in our wildest dreams would have ever predicted that. Jon said,

"It's like we're kids on top of a hill watching a snowball just roll down the hill completely out of control. It's staggering." Following the success of this movie, God began to open doors that no man could open.

As these doors opened, Andy and Jon started asking, "What can we do together that none of us can do alone? Is there a way, instead of being soloists, that we can become a symphony?" The more they asked these questions, the more the questions became a dream, which led them to recruit some talented people they were dying to work with. This led them to focus on creating a Christian movie studio. Could they leverage their success from *I Can Only Imagine* to form a new faith-based studio?

As the days and weeks passed, their dream started to become a reality when they were approached by Lionsgate, which would distribute the films. After months of negotiations in the summer of 2018, Lionsgate offered them an unbelievable deal. Under the headline "Lionsgate Signs Multi-Platform Film and Television First-Look Deal with the Erwin Brothers and Kevin Downes," part of the release read:

> "We're proud to expand our relationship with Andrew, Jon, and Kevin through this exciting and collaborative cross-divisional partnership," said [chairman Joe] Drake and [television group chairman Kevin] Beggs. "This deal underscores our ongoing commitment to serve moviegoers with premium, faith-based content. We look forward to working with the Erwin Brothers and Kevin on film and television projects that resonate not only with the faith-based community but with viewers everywhere."[1]

Now what? Andy and Jon said they felt they had been "stewarded with an incredible moment that gave us incredible leverage, influence, and opportunity."[2]

The next months were filled with meetings and planning for the next step. Andy, Jon, and their production partners, Kevin Downes and Tony Young, were busy forming a new filmmaking studio, which would bring multiple filmmakers together to create a pipeline of event movies that would proclaim a biblical message.

But how and when would they reveal the details of their new plan? The answer became clear: They would reveal this on March 27, 2019, in Anaheim, California, at the National Religious Broadcasters Christian Media Convention. The plan was for the Kingdom Story Company's launch event to be an incredible multimedia presentation that would be livestreamed on Facebook and made available to more than fifty million people!

Six months of planning went into their keynote event, one of the biggest announcements ever made in terms of Christian cinema.

"If you see further," Jon said, "it's because you stand on the shoulders of giants. There has been such a great foundation laid in Christian film. There are those moments when there is a quantum leap forward and you get to be a part of it."

This announcement was to be one of those moments. It was going to involve building a multiple-screen set so the team could present their dream.

The day of the event arrived. At 3:45 p.m., Hank and I left the greenroom to take our seats in the front row. As the crowd began to gather in the large auditorium, the atmosphere was electric. The room was soon full, and then people began to fill the overflow room. The middle screen displayed the new logo, and then the five-foot countdown numbers appeared on that screen. As the music became more intense and the number reached ten, everyone started counting out loud: "Ten, nine, eight, seven . . ." Finally, Jon took center stage to begin the two-hour extravaganza.

> "We're here to dream, as my dad always told us, to 'dream bold, dream big, dream the impossible,'" Jon said. "We've been dreaming of this for a long time. This dream is ten years in the making!
>
> "What can we do together that none of us can do alone? Is there a way, instead of being soloists, that we can become a symphony? That's why today, this new team is here to make a major announcement and to launch that dream. We're not here to launch a movie. We're here to launch a movie studio."[3]

As the multimedia presentation continued, the heartbeat of this new dream would become crystal clear as everyone was introduced to some of the new Kingdom Story Company team members.

> "Our dream for launching Kingdom is to create the most trusted and respected brand in faith-based entertainment. We needed a partner that would catch that dream with us, and Lionsgate is the perfect fit," Jon said. "They aren't like any other studio we've ever worked with, and they have a passion to empower

creative entrepreneurs. We can't wait to work together on some exciting new projects."

Kevin said, "This is not about us. It's about a bigger vision and bringing together artists around the country that are believers, that share the same passion that we do. We want to give them a platform to really speak."

Tony said, "I love the way the Lord has blessed this dream. A place where creatives can come and we can incubate their talent to really generate some great content."

Andy added, "Our creative ambition and directing sweet spot is to tell redemptive, inspirational stories that appeal to audiences everywhere. We need optimism and hope more than ever today, and those are the stories we love to tell."[4]

What a worth-it moment for this mom, and what a reminder that I am only part of this masterpiece. I had only been a brush in the hand of a powerful God. But I hadn't been the only brush: He had used many brushes. You see, God had given my sons His creative ambition. He had prepared them for His dream for such a day as this, and the story has only just begun.

Just a reminder to you, Mom. You must be willing to be His brush, but you must also remind yourself that He will use many brushes to paint your dreamer's masterpiece, and you must respond to that fact with humility and gratefulness.

PART TWO

Foundations

*So everyone who hears these words of Mine
and acts upon them [obeying them] will be like a
sensible (prudent, practical, wise) man who built
his house upon the rock. And the rain fell and the
floods came and the winds blew and beat against
that house; yet it did not fall, because it had been
founded on the rock. And everyone who hears
these words of Mine and does not do them will be
like a stupid (foolish) man who built his house upon
the sand. And the rain fell and the floods came and
the winds blew and beat against that house, and
it fell—and great and complete was the fall of it.*

MATTHEW 7:24-27

FOUNDATION 1:

Watch and Learn

THE YEAR WAS 1977. I was in my late twenties. My husband and I did not have children yet, and I was working as the principal of a small Christian school in Dallas. I learned so much about being a parent while observing the parents of the children in that school. And even though there were many parents and students from whom I learned a great deal, it was meetings with two sets of parents that profoundly changed my views on parenting and on life forever.

The daughter of the first set of parents proved exceptional in the classroom. She was highly intelligent, diligent, and for the most part, extremely obedient. She never made anything less than 100 percent on any of her work. As the year progressed, I observed that her behavior on the playground did not match her behavior in the classroom. She always wanted to win, and when she didn't, she would have an abrupt meltdown. She did not know how to cope with failure. As was my custom, when I noticed that a child at the school was having difficulty in any area, I invited the parents to talk with me.

I began our session with all the positive things I saw in their daughter. First, I spoke of her great success within the classroom. We then discussed my concern with her handling of failure. I suggested that they might want to find activities outside of school for her to participate in that afforded her opportunities to learn to fail graciously. Observing their facial expressions, a person would have thought I had just asked them to take their child outside and shoot her. It was obvious they did not appreciate my input and were not pleased with my suggestions. I knew when they left my office that day that nothing would change. In fact, they did not enroll their daughter the following year.

Another set of parents also had a child who was doing quite well in the classroom, but as the year progressed, I noticed that their child had an argumentative spirit. If I said the sky was blue, she would say, "Well, it's really a lavender color." She was constantly correcting everyone around her. Despite the fear in my heart of another negative parental response, I contacted her parents for a conference.

The mother arrived that day alone with pen and notebook in her hand. The father was not able to come because he was in seminary classes working toward his doctorate. To say I was a little intimidated by this meeting would be an understatement. I began the same process, telling this mom what I had seen in her child. She asked me to give her some examples, and I provided three or four. As she listened to me, she wrote them down in her notebook.

When she got up to leave, she turned to me and said, "Thank you so much for loving my daughter enough to let me know about this." She assured me that she and her husband would discuss the situation that night and get back to me in the next few days.

Two days later she contacted me with a report of the activities that had taken place in her home. She shared something with me that I'll never forget. Her first statement was, "We had a revival at our house." She further explained that she sat down with her husband and reviewed the list she had made at school that day. She shared that as she read, she heard her husband quietly crying as he sat next to her. He said, "I'm the problem. I have an argumentative spirit. As you began to tell me what the principal shared, the Lord convicted me about it." They prayed together that night, and he asked for the Lord's forgiveness. They asked the Lord to change his heart, and he promised to work on getting rid of this in his own life.

They then called their daughter down to the living room to talk. This precious, godly father poured his heart out to his daughter that night. He told her that he had confessed his sin to the Lord and now he needed to ask her forgiveness for being a bad example. He then told her she needed to deal with her own sin as well.

That Spirit-filled, Christ-centered mom told me that they had come up with a plan to help her daughter remember not to argue. If I heard her daughter being argumentative, I would place a hand on her shoulder, and my gentle touch would remind her of her sin. She called it *sin*. This was to remind her that she was not to argue but instead stop and change her attitude. The mom thanked me again, and we said good-bye.

I only had to place my hand on their daughter's shoulder twice. In the weeks that followed, I saw the little girl begin to choose righteousness instead of sin. She was changing, and it was glorious to witness. That was the day I said, "I want to be that kind of parent!"

My fellow mom, I want to encourage you to set your heart and mind to be ever learning from both God and His people about how to be the best mom to your dreamer. I am so grateful to the Lord for allowing me to see the transforming power of Christ in a family committed to representing the glory of God. It gave me such hope. I reasoned that if God could do it for them, then He could do it for all of us. He can also do it for you and your dreamer.

FOUNDATION 2:

"Any Old Bush Will Do"

IN SEPTEMBER 1978, GOD GIFTED US with a sweet, blond-headed, blue-eyed baby boy. As I always had planned, I began my new occupation as a full-time mom. Running a school was a piece of cake compared to being a full-time mom. I felt so inadequate. As an only child, I had not been around many babies growing up. This new task overwhelmed me.

When my son Andy was about nine months old, I stood over his crib, watched him sleep, and cried out to God with my whole heart. I remembered Mrs. Yancey, my Bible teacher and mentor for many years, telling me about a prayer she had prayed over her children. It was simple yet powerful. Standing over Andy's crib, I prayed to the Lord, "Oh, Father, will You protect Andy from my flesh—my old sin nature, my lack of wisdom, just me? Will You parent my children through me? Here I am—use me, teach me; here are my ears, mouth, eyes, and hands—all yielded to You." There began the quest of parenthood for me.

There were many times I was sure God had given my sons

the wrong mom, but I can say He was faithful to me and them as well. The late Major Ian Thomas, an evangelical writer, theological teacher, and founder of the Torchbearers Bible schools, was known to say, "Any old bush will do."[1] There was nothing special about the burning bush through which God spoke to Moses. It was not the bush that mattered, but what was *in* the bush. I told the Lord that I would be more than happy to be His burning bush through which He could parent my son.

> Now Moses kept the flock of Jethro his father-in-law,
> the priest of Midian; and he led the flock to the back
> or west side of the wilderness and came to Horeb or
> Sinai, the mountain of God. The Angel of the Lord
> appeared to him in a flame of fire out of the midst of
> a bush; and he looked, and behold, the bush burned
> with fire, yet was not consumed. And Moses said, I will
> now turn aside and see this great sight, why the bush
> is not burned. And when the Lord saw that he turned
> aside to see, God called to him out of the midst of the
> bush and said, Moses, Moses! And he said, Here am I.
> EXODUS 3:1-4

I have come to understand that good, diligent parents use one of two child-raising methods. I call them *limited parenting* and *unlimited parenting*.

Parents using the *limited-parenting* method work hard at being good parents. They may read every book ever written on the subject. Most likely they will work hard to make sure that they give their children every advantage. They may worry about what they are doing or not doing to develop their child's potential. By most standards, they are very good parents. As good as that may be, and as hard as they work, their parenting is limited. It is limited to their human effort, knowledge, potential, and understanding of each of their children.

On the other hand, to all born-again Christian parents there's the option of *unlimited parenting*. This method of parenting is only limited to a parent's willingness to give Christ unlimited control. Parents who use this method will most likely do all or more of the things parents who use limited parenting do, except worry, with one important difference. Instead of parents being limited to their own human abilities and understanding, they have access to God's unlimited abilities and His unlimited understanding of the heart of each of their children.

Many times, I've cried out to God for wisdom and understanding of my sons. I have also remarked to other parents, "I don't have a clue as to what to do about your child, but I know God does." Christ Jesus knows all about them, and He has promised us wisdom. Scripture says that He not only gives us wisdom, but He gives it liberally (see James 1:5). And by the way, it also says He gives it to everyone who understands that they are deficient in wisdom and then asks for it.

Unlimited parenting must rely a great deal on example, similar to when Paul said to his disciples, "Pattern yourselves after me [follow my example], as I imitate and follow Christ (the Messiah)" (1 Corinthians 11:1). In other words, he was saying, "I want you to watch the way I walk and walk just like me. Watch what I do, how I keep my heart clean. Watch how I yield. Watch how I obey. Watch what I do when I blow it. Watch me." As believing parents, we are to say to our little ones, our disciples, "Jesus dwells in us, and because He has made it so, we can walk in His power. Watch me and follow me as I follow Jesus."

In order to be a parent who uses the unlimited method of parenting (one who is totally dependent on Christ to parent your children), you must yield all that you are to the control of the Lord God Almighty. You must allow His life to parent through you in the power of the Holy Spirit. Then and only then will you not be limited to your own parenting. You may give your child the best advantage of all, a relationship with Jesus. Believe me, Jesus can be a better parent to your children than you could ever hope to be.

FOUNDATION 3:

Recognize "But God" Moments

WHAT ARE "BUT GOD" MOMENTS, and how can we learn to recognize them? Learning to recognize them is as foundational as learning to follow God. Scripture is full of the phrase "but God," and it refers to many different scenarios. It can refer to a miracle that only God can do. Sometimes things are not going well, and God steps in to save the day. Or "but God" may refer to a change of direction.

One of my favorite scenes in *Woodlawn* is near the end of the movie when someone says, "Do you believe in miracles?" A character named Tandy says, "Yes, I do. I am one."[1]

Well, I'm just Shelia, and I do believe in miracles, because I am one. I'm just a girl who was born in Gadsden, Alabama, just a girl who eventually learned to recognize the "but God" moments of life. "But God" moments can be for provision, protection, or just direction. It's important that we allow God to be in charge, to recognize the "but God" moments, and adjust our lives to His will. Then we need to teach our children to do the same thing.

My Beginning with God

When I was six years old, our small church had a revival. On a warm March Sunday night, I acted by faith in what I heard, and I became God's child forever.

Although I don't remember much about starting my new life in Christ, I know I was grateful for His dying for me. I also thought it was now up to me to pay Him back by being the best Christian I could be. Every time we had a revival, I rededicated my life to Christ. My purpose was to please God and to "be good."

Through heartache and disappointment, I came to the end of myself and my own effort to live the Christian life. I was twenty years old when I understood I could not be what I wanted to be. I found my heart attitudes were still a problem, and I was helpless to do anything about them. In disappointment and frustration, I told the Lord that I could not live the Christian life and that if this was the abundant life, I didn't want it. The Lord began to teach me that He never said I could live the Christian life. By studying His Word, I began to understand that He is the only one who can live the Christian life, and He will live it through me, if I only yield to His control.

This was the best news I had ever heard. I did yield! My life has never been the same. He has done more than I could ever have dreamed of or hoped for. His love is from everlasting to everlasting—what a Savior! Not only did He live a perfect life for me and then die on the cross for me; He continues to live His life through me. In return, I get to experience a truly abundant life, as John 10:10 says: "The thief comes only in order to steal and kill and destroy. I came that they may have and enjoy life, and have it in abundance."

By that time, I had graduated from high school and was attending college, where I met and married Hank. Long before we met, we had both committed our lives to full-time Christian work. Together we have spent more than forty-seven years in a variety of ministries, and we have experienced many "but God" moments as we've followed the Lord's direction for our lives and guided our sons to do the same.

Our "But God" Moments

Our story is one of many "but God" moments. God had a plan not only for us but for our dreamer sons as well. As you walk through life you may not see what God is doing or even why He is directing your life the way He is, but as you follow Him by faith, later it may become very clear. We learned that He was not just directing us; He was putting our sons in just the right place to be able to follow His plan for them.

As college seniors, my husband and I thought we would go on staff with Campus Crusade for Christ (Cru) after graduation because we'd been Cru leaders during college, *but God* had different plans for us, so we moved to Birmingham to start over again.

We moved into a small one-bedroom apartment while Hank continued his education at Southeastern Bible College and I taught school. Hank also worked part-time as a church youth director. What an unbelievable year 1972 was for Hank and me! In the early seventies God was sweeping our nation with a youth revival, the Jesus Movement, by which we saw many lives transformed through our ministry.

That fall the Lord gave me a wonderful gift. Soon after I communicated to Hank my ongoing struggle to apply all the things I had learned about being a godly wife, he learned about a lady teaching a Bible study in our city. The next week, I met Joyce Yancey, speaker and Bible teacher with the Wales Goebel Ministry, a ministry to teenagers in Birmingham. Over the past forty-six years she has been my spiritual mom and mentor. Watching her walk with the Lord through some hard times grew my faith and trust in Him.

At the end of that year, Wales Goebel, founder of the ministry named for him, invited us to join his team. We were assigned Woodlawn High School. The next two years were filled with revival in a school torn apart by the adjustment to integration, but we watched God show up! (Hank would later tell Andy and Jon bedtime stories about his adventures at Woodlawn High School. They began to dream about making a movie about the Woodlawn football team. Hank was just having fun telling them these stories. He had no idea what God was doing in his sons' little hearts. In 2015, there it was: Hank's story on the big screen, the movie *Woodlawn*. I call that a "but God" moment. Mom, you never know what God is planting in your dreamers' hearts as they watch your life unfold.)

Hank's dream was to attend Dallas Theological Seminary. In 1975 their freshman class was full, but Hank was accepted to summer school, so off we went to Dallas with our little car packed to the top with our belongings. I thought the plan would be to return to Birmingham at the end of that summer. *But God* had a different plan.

Not many people stayed in Dallas for summer school, so it was a long, lonely summer. I got a summer job working at a fabric store, but I was homesick and longed to be back in Birmingham with our great friends. Every single day on my way home from work I asked the Lord to let us go home to Birmingham. One day I noticed a vacant apartment for rent next door to the apartment that we were subleasing for the summer. In my heart, I was hoping that someone would rent that apartment so we wouldn't have a place to live and would have to move back to Birmingham to once again be with all our friends and family. Sure enough, one afternoon I came by that apartment and the rent sign was gone. I thought to myself, *We're going home!* When I walked into our apartment, Hank was standing there grinning from ear to ear. He shared that he had gotten a spot in the freshman class at the last minute and that he'd rented the apartment.

And it wasn't long before I began to fall in love with Dallas. God gave us many wonderful friends, and we lived in Dallas for the following seven years.

To make ends meet, Hank secured a job working at the radio station at First Baptist Dallas. He was a natural and fell in love with radio work. In December of that year we found ourselves in a new place of learning to trust God. We did not have the money for Hank's winter semester of school. We prayed and Hank even enrolled, but when school began, the money was not there and he dropped out. It did not make sense. Why? *But God* had a plan. In January, a local TV station asked Hank to work for them. Hank replied, "I don't know anything about being a news reporter." They said, "We'll train you." (This was the beginning of the world of cameras and editing that would lead our sons into the world of filmmaking.)

There was a good reason that God had not provided the money for Hank to go to school that winter. I was pregnant and would not be going back to work in September so I could become a full-time stay-at-home mom. God had provided even before we knew we had a need. After Hank worked a couple of years as a reporter, the TV station asked him to become an anchor. At that point Hank could have returned to finish his degree at Dallas Theological Seminary, and Hank and I were in love with Dallas. It looked like it would be our forever home, *but God* was about to send us back to Birmingham.

While we were in Birmingham for a dear friend's wedding, Hank got a call from a station in Birmingham, the "Magic City." Channel 42 TV needed an anchor and news director, and they wanted Hank. We spent the next two weeks packing to return to Alabama. (Andy would go to the station with Hank and sit on set with him. Little did we know that God was beginning to show Andy a whole new world.)

As you can see, our story is a story of *but God*. With many more twists and turns, Hank accepted a job as the host of a talk radio show that lasted twenty years. He became the Christian conservative voice for most of the state of Alabama. I remained a stay-at-home mom, community Bible teacher, and home-school teacher for our sons. (Homeschooling was important to our sons for a lot of reasons. "But God" led this way so there would be Erwin Brothers Entertainment. Andy is four years older than Jon, and had they been in public school, their worlds would have been very far apart. But with homeschooling, they did everything together, and they began to dream about making movies as a team.)

Our sons finished high school and life was good. *But God*, in the winter of 1999, provided a new surprise in our lives. A chance encounter changed our direction once again. As Hank congratulated a friend and state senator on his upcoming run for lieutenant governor, he asked him who was running for his seat in the senate. The man responded, "How about you?" When Hank told me about the conversation, I said I thought it was a great idea. After going to our pastor, our sons, and both of our parents, and receiving a green light from all of them, Hank decided to run for the seat.

The night before the election, Hank and I felt God was going to give Hank the victory. We did not tell anyone else about that evening. The day after the election, the newspaper headlines read, "Miracle ERWIN Wins Senate Seat." For the next eight years Hank became Senator Erwin. All the years of training in his role at his radio show equipped him for this opportunity, and God mightily used him.

God has planned for wonderful "but God" moments in *your* life also, as you find and grow your child's God-given talents. As you have seen in our story, not only was God showing up for us, but He was also using all of those "but God" moments to direct our sons' lives as well. So keep your eyes open, because He will do the same for you and your dreamers. Proverbs 16:9 says, "A man's mind plans his way [as he journeys through life], but the LORD directs his steps and establishes them" (AMP).

PART THREE

Essentials

For His divine power has bestowed on us
[absolutely] everything necessary for [a
dynamic spiritual] life and godliness, through
true and personal knowledge of Him who
called us by His own glory and excellence.

2 PETER 1:3, AMP

ESSENTIAL 1:

Embrace Your Faith

IF YOU ARE WANTING TO RAISE UP your dreamers to follow God's plan for their lives, you must first know what you believe and then teach that to your dreamer. Your dreamers cannot connect with their callings from the Lord if they do not know Him.

Hank and I determined that the sole purpose of our family was to get to know the Lord Jesus Christ and to make Him known. We resolved to do only those things that pleased Him and caused people to want to know Him too.

Our family's purpose statement is "To know Him (Jesus) and make Him known." Our family's purpose verse is:

[For my determined purpose is] that I may know
Him [that I may progressively become more deeply
and intimately acquainted with Him, perceiving and
recognizing and understanding the wonders of His
Person more strongly and more clearly], and that
I may in that same way come to know the power
outflowing from His resurrection [which it exerts over

believers], and that I may so share His sufferings as to be continually transformed [in spirit into His likeness even] to His death, [in the hope] that if possible I may attain to the [spiritual and moral] resurrection [that lifts me] out from among the dead [even while in the body].

PHILIPPIANS 3:10-11

This is my favorite Bible verse. It starts with "That I may know Him." How have we applied this to our lives?

I believe that the sole purpose of Christianity is found in this verse. Shouldn't our goal be to know Him and make Him known? God always starts with the individual. Every member of our family has to have an individual relationship with the Lord Jesus Christ. Moms, it must start with you! You cannot share an experience you haven't had. If you try to do that, your children will call it what it is: hypocrisy. Your purpose must be to get to know Him and then to make Him known to your children. God has no grandchildren, only children. We must see that our witness must be unto Him, for Him, and about Him, starting where we are. For us, dear moms, that means our witness begins with our own children! Then you can reach out to others outside of your home.

Knowing and pleasing Jesus, not people, is our goal. We never told our children they had to be obedient because Daddy was in the ministry or because other people were watching. We taught them the reason for their obedience is because it pleases the Lord. As you follow Christ, they will learn to follow Christ as well.

Philippians 3:10-11 tells us that we must get to know Jesus, progressively more deeply and intimately, by seeing the wonder of His person strongly and more clearly. *Progressively* we grow, recognizing and understanding Him through His Word. Our goal is to always go deeper in faith and to share it with those around us through the overflowing life that indwells us.

Major Ian Thomas questions in his book *The Indwelling Life of Christ,*

> Do you know what it is to live purposefully? Is there an urgent sense of mission or some compelling thrust within you which makes life add up to the sheer adventure that God always intended life to be?
>
> Or are you simply engaged in the struggle for existence and survival?
>
> Worse still, have you been caught up into the rat race of competitive existence? Haunted by the fear of being overtaken by others at the next bend in the road? Breathlessly trying to keep up with events that travel faster than your capacity to cope with them?[1]

Our sons have found their meaning and purpose because they have embraced a relationship with Jesus. Their work is infused with this purpose: to know Him and to make Him known.

As we discover our dreamers' God-given talents, we must teach them to embrace their faith so they can discover God's plan for their lives and how He wants them to use their gifts for the Kingdom.

ESSENTIAL 2:

Make Jesus Your Standard

WE SHOULD LIVE OUR LIVES in such a way that there is no explanation for the way we live except our relationship with Jesus. Making sure our family feels special is indispensably important, but the most important thing is to make sure every member of our family feels special because of their relationship to Jesus.

The world continues to be outrageous around us, but we must do all we can to create and maintain a Christ-centered home where everything is done is for God's glory. Scripture encourages us to have a home where even angels would feel welcome!

I remember looking at my sons when they were small and thinking, *Who are you? What is God's plan for you?* I am not as proud of what they do as of who they are. I love that they love the Lord and love their wives and children well.

Jesus Christ must be our standard for all things—and most preciously, our greatest adviser for mothering. To keep Jesus as our standard and become like Him, we need to stay connected to Him. Let me explain with a story. In 1986, when I was forty, we moved into the first house that we actually owned. I remember one morning standing at my sink looking out at my beautiful backyard. It was springtime, and everything was beginning to bloom. As I looked at the back corner of our yard, I realized that we had a beautiful apple tree. I love green apples, so to me the tree in my backyard that would bear green apples for me to eat in the fall was truly a gift from God. That tree reminded me of a truth I'd been taught about bearing fruit in my life as a Christian.

What if I invited you over to see the beautiful tree? Next, just before you came, what if I ran to the store and bought some large green apples and some red velvet ribbon? Then I took the red ribbon and tied the green apples to the tree? I'm sure when you got to my house and saw the green apples hanging from the red ribbon you would think I was a little crazy. The sad part about the green apples is that in a few days they would begin to die, not really being connected to the tree.

On the other hand, if I just waited, the lovely white blossoms on my tree would eventually fall off and in their place would be tiny little apples. These tiny little apples would slowly begin to grow. By September I would have a tree full of fresh, juicy green apples.

What was the difference between the two kinds of apples? The first apples just hung on the tree, and the second apples were connected to the tree. All winter long something had been going on inside the tree, and because of that, the tree was full of lovely sweet-smelling apple blossoms on a beautiful spring morning. The Christian life is just like that apple tree. The

Spirit of God lives in us and is doing things inside us that eventually will bud on the outside. As we are yielded to Him, He will begin to produce holiness in our lives, and that will help us raise dreamers for God. I pray that you want your dreamer to experience a life yielded to God and therefore will want their gifts to bring glory to Him.

ESSENTIAL 3:

Follow the Supreme Authority

THE BIBLE IS THE SUPREME AUTHORITY. We need to study it, learn it, and submit ourselves to its principles and its commands. If the above statement is true, and it is, we need to know it and then teach it to our dreamers. They need to know what the truth is in order to know how to navigate life and follow God's path for their lives.

> But the Word of the Lord (divine instruction, the Gospel) endures forever. And this Word is the good news which was preached to you.
> I PETER 1:25

> Every Scripture is God-breathed (given by His inspiration) and profitable for instruction, for reproof and conviction of sin, for correction of error and discipline in obedience, [and] for training in righteousness (in holy living, in conformity to God's will in thought, purpose, and action), so that the man

of God may be complete and proficient, well fitted
and thoroughly equipped for every good work.
2 TIMOTHY 3:16-17

The Bible is our instruction manual for life! A young man
took his test to get his driver's permit at the same time as
another young man. The second young man didn't pass the
test and afterward asked the first young man how he did so well.
The first man said, "I studied the instruction book until I knew
it backward and forward." Much to my amusement, the other
young man asked, "You mean there was an instruction book?"

I'm afraid this is the way a lot of Christians approach the
Christian life. They don't know what God expects of them
because they do not study the Bible.

That young man had to study the instruction book to pass
his test. He also had to take a driver's test. In that test, the
instructor got to see how well he had learned to submit himself
to what he had learned in the book. We as Christians must
not only know the Bible, but we must submit ourselves to its
principles.

When we lived in Dallas, Hank thought it would be fun
to umpire some baseball games, so he went to umpire school.
Hank said, "Before the season started, we had a regional meeting with all the umpires in the district. The special guest was the
head umpire in the district, with years of experience. He held
up a copy of the rule book and said, 'Men, this is the rule book!
Memorize it! Eat it! Drink it! Dream it! Know it inside and out!
Because when you are on the field in the middle of the game
and tempers are flying, everyone in the stadium will think they
know the rules! But you may be the only one in the whole park

who really knows what the rules really say and what they really mean! Memorize the book!' And he sat down."

This is how we should approach the Bible. As a mom, I tried to teach my boys to love the Word of God and to obey Jesus. Real joy and life are found in Jesus, and we can get to know Him by reading His book.

What is required of me since the Bible is supreme? Obedience that is prompt, with no debate, and I must be persistent as well.

As a parent, wouldn't you like your children to just obey you because they love you? Jesus said if you love Him, then obey Him.

Mom, your dreamers must know what God has said about how to live life in order to find their purposes. Since God gave them their abilities, He has the right to say how they are to use their gifts. To live a truly successful life, it must be lived God's way. It's so important for you to know the Word of God so you can teach it to your dreamer.

When our sons had a question about life, we always started by asking, "What does the Bible say about the subject?" Then when we found out, we adjusted our lives to what it said. That is what obedience is.

ESSENTIAL 4:

Live Holy

HOLINESS IS THE HABIT OF BEING of one mind with God! It means hating what God hates, loving what He loves, and measuring everything by His standard (His Word). What does holiness have to do with being a mom who raises dreamers for God? Well, you cannot view your child in the correct way until you have seen Jesus for who He is and yourself for who you are. You must understand that Jesus has made you clean, and you must see your God as a holy, loving, transforming God. You must know that God can train you in holy living and that you can train your children in that same holy lifestyle. You have to know that Jesus is their only hope because He is your only hope. You must see your children through the eyes of Jesus, who is the only One who can show you what your children truly need. You must see that you are a sinner in need of a Savior and that your children are sinners in need of a Savior. This is not just so they can get to heaven but also so they can live a holy, godly life.

With that in mind, let's see what the Bible says about holy

living. Isaiah 6 is one of my favorite passages about holiness. It's one of those passages that God has made true in my own life. Isaiah 6:1 says, "In the year that King Uzziah died I saw the Lord sitting upon a throne, high and lifted up; and the train of his robe filled the temple" (ESV).

The throne of Judah was empty; the king was dead. At that point Isaiah saw the King of kings and the Lord of lords. Israel's king was dead, but Isaiah's God was still alive. The throne was empty. Nobody was in control. But *God* was still very much in control. What did Isaiah see that day? He saw his King high and lifted up above all the other kings. He saw the Ruler of all still upon His throne, the glory of God still in control, and a sovereign God who never changes. He saw a holy, all-knowing, all-powerful God whose train filled the Temple from top to bottom. Back in those days, the more elaborate a king's robe and train were, the more power and wealth he had.

Years ago, I had the privilege of sewing a wedding dress for my dear friend's daughter. Every time I think about this verse, I think about the moment we attached her gorgeous train that filled my living room floor. The train only filled my living room floor. That is not what this particular passage means. God's train totally filled the Temple, from the bottom to the top. It was stuffed in with no space left. It appeared packed in, complete, reflecting His power, authority, and wealth. Isaiah's God, the true King of kings, was still in control even when the earthly throne was empty. What hope!

Above Him stood the seraphim; each had six wings:
with two [each] covered his [own] face, and with two
[each] covered his feet, and with two [each] flew. And

one cried to another and said, Holy, holy, holy is the
Lord of hosts; the whole earth is full of His glory!

ISAIAH 6:2-3

The seraphim, or holy angels, surrounded His throne. They
each had six wings, but the wings were not stretched upward.
Four were used for covering: two were used for covering the
face, and two were used for covering their feet. They were
showing humility and reverence as they cried to one another,
"Holy, holy, holy." They did not cry *holy* once or even twice.
No, they cried, "Holy, holy, holy." I have read that the reason
the term *holy* was used three times was in reference to the
three persons of the Godhead—Holy Father, Holy Son, and
Holy Spirit. The use of *holy* three times was most likely used
to show just how holy God is. His holiness is complete, and
He is completely holy.

Isaiah not only saw the glory and holiness; he also saw the
power of the Lord, a power mighty enough to shake foundations. Isaiah 6:4 says, "And the foundations of the thresholds
shook at the voice of him who cried, and the house was filled
with smoke."

The very foundation shook at God's voice; the posts of the
door were shaken by His voice. That was the same voice that
spoke the world into existence. Everything obeyed Him. What
authority! How glorious! This is a reminder: If there's anything
in my life that needs God's power, He has the power to change
me. This is the same voice the disciples heard during the storm
that terrified them. They cried out to Jesus, and He just turned
around and said, "Stop." Even the wind obeys His voice.

Is there anything in your life that needs His power?

Remember that He is your Father and also the all-powerful God. Isn't that exciting? My friend's sister lives in California and experienced an earthquake. She says she cannot begin to explain the terror she felt when the earth moved, and she realized the power of God is still able to shake the earth. What would your reaction be to something like this?

When I was younger, in my late twenties, it seemed like God taught me one truth a year. It wasn't that I didn't learn other things; it just seemed everything revolved around whatever main lesson He was teaching me at the time. The year my father died, God began to show me He really is *God*. An amazing, supernatural, wonderful, all-knowing, omnipresent, just, loving, merciful, gracious, and powerful God. The kind of God who makes you want to fall on your face before Him and worship.

Some of my friends asked me, "What's God teaching you?" My reply was, "That He is God." They looked at me like I had two heads. I could see they were thinking, *Poor girl, does she not know that by now?*

When Isaiah took a long look up, he saw his God for who He really is, and he saw something else as well. He took an honest look inward and saw himself ruined and unclean in comparison. Have you ever noticed how your husband's older undershirts seem clean and white until you place new white undershirts next to them in the drawer? Isaiah, when compared to the cleanness of God, found out he was unclean. So he cried out, "Woe is me! For I am undone and ruined, because I am a man of unclean lips" (Isaiah 6:5).

This was an honest assessment. It was a short look in, not a pity party. We cannot look too far inward and end up thinking that God could never use us. You don't want to have these thoughts: *I'm awful. You don't understand. If you just knew me.* That thinking is nothing more than pride in reverse (nevertheless, sinful pride). Pride is self-centeredness. When I'm sitting around feeling sorry for myself and talking about how horrible I am, pride is my problem. God already said that about us. He said we deserve to go to hell, but He also said He would change that destiny. Look to God, who is holy, holy, holy, whose train filled the Temple. Are you too challenging for Him? I don't think so! Isn't that what you're saying if you say you are too horrible? A girl actually told me that once. She said, "I see all these other women being transformed, but I'm just too bad for God to change."

Isaiah's "woe is me" expression is an honest, repentant spirit. It says, "God, I am what You say I am. I'm wicked. I don't love anyone but myself. When given the opportunity, I will choose wickedness over holiness every time. I am undone and powerless to change myself." One thing we need to remember about repentance is that we shouldn't make excuses for living unchanged by God, in sin. Sometimes we think we do what we do because of things that have happened to us in the past. We blame our circumstances. The truth is, our responses all come from within us.

Joyce Yancey used to teach it this way: If I invited you over to my house for tea, brought out my beautiful teacups and put a tea bag in your cup, then poured hot water over it, what would happen? In a short while you would have a hot cup of tea. What made the tea? Was it the tea in the bag or was it the hot water? All the hot water did was draw out the tea that was already in the bag. It was there all along. We must take personal responsibility for all our sin. If we responded incorrectly, no matter what the circumstances, the issue is not the hot water. The thing that happened to you just drew out of you what was already there.

The reason Jesus wants to draw out the unpleasant parts inside us is so we can deal with it all, so we can really see what's inside. Then we can allow Him to deal properly and ruthlessly with our sin. You can take even your darkest parts to Him. We can cry out, even as Isaiah did, "Woe is me!" We can say, "I'm broken, absolutely broken." Isaiah's cry was an honest evaluation with a repentant spirit. We can say God is right about who I am. I'm wicked. I don't blame anyone but myself. Even my good is self-righteous. "I'm undone," Isaiah said. "I'm without hope."

Have you ever recognized the Lord in the Word of God as the Holy One? Did it cause you to see yourself for who you really are? You are sinful and broken, but remember, God is certainly capable of using broken things. The little boy who had the lunch basket and gave it to Jesus had no idea that He would feed five thousand men that day. Scripture says Jesus blessed the bread, and after He broke it and gave it away, there was more left over. It's in our brokenness that God can use us. It's in that difficulty, that hard spot, that we can see ourselves as we really are and God as He really is.

What is the difference between a prideful, unbroken person and a broken person? A proud person focuses on the failures of others. A broken person is overwhelmed with her own spiritual need and truly cares about the needs of others.

We do not see visions like Isaiah did as a prophet of old, but we have the Bible to show us what our God is really like. Our response should be the same as Isaiah's response: We are unclean sinners! We are lost, ruined, without hope.

Isaiah said his lips were unclean. Why would he specify that body part? Scripture tells us that out of the heart the mouth speaks. Isaiah's heart was unclean. It would be sad if the Scripture stopped here—with the glory of God and the ruined state of man. Praise God that it does not!

One seraph flew to Isaiah with a live coal, and he touched Isaiah's lips. The burning coal took care of three things: iniquity, wicked acts, and guilt. These three things were atoned for and forgiven. *Atone* means to cover over. To *forgive* means to send away completely, to cancel, to remove the cause of the offense.

In Hebrews 10 we can see the difference between Old Testament atonement for sin through the offering of animals as a sacrifice and forgiveness of our sins achieved through Jesus Christ's death on the cross. The first part of the chapter tells us of the work of the Old Testament priest who offered lambs and goats to atone for the sins of God's people. However, this could not make perfect those who approached the altar.

For since the Law has merely a rude outline (foreshadowing) of the good things to come—instead of fully expressing those things—it can never by offering the same sacrifices continually year after year make perfect those who approach [its altars].

HEBREWS 10:1

The law could not make people perfect—so now we have a problem! Adam and Eve were made in the image of God— perfect. They had full fellowship with God. They had all their needs met by God and a perfect mate. In the Garden they were without sin, but Eve chose to disobey God, and Adam followed her. They were no longer perfect. Paradise was lost and they were cast out.

How terribly sad is this story in Genesis 3. There was a perfect man in a perfect place with the perfect mate and a perfect relationship with the God of the universe. God walked with him in the Garden. On this day when God came to have fellowship with Adam and Eve, He found that they were hiding. They were hiding because they were guilty and ashamed, but the saddest reason was that for the first time, they were afraid to be in the presence of God. His glory that clothed them in the Garden was gone. They knew they were naked, and they were ashamed.

They made for themselves aprons to cover their nakedness. This was man's first attempt to take care of his own sin. God in His mercy and love spoke that day. He asked the question that He still asks to this day of His creation: "Where are you?" That day in the Garden, we see the first animal blood shed to cover Adam and Eve's nakedness. We see the mercy of God casting them out of the Garden and having the seraphim guard the entrance so that they could not eat of the tree of life. And yes, that act is mercy, because if they had eaten of that tree, they would have remained in their sin forever. God had a plan to redeem man, and the shedding of blood was just a picture of things to come.

Has anyone ever asked you if you know the price of getting into heaven? Well, the answer is "perfection." God is holy. He cannot look at sin and cannot allow sin to be a part of heaven, so to get into heaven you must be perfect. If you or I can be perfect (holy, morally blameless, free from sin, separated from sin), we can go to heaven when we die in this world. There is a problem, though. Romans 3:23 says that "all have sinned and fall short of the glory of God" (ESV).

So how can we live in heaven if we can never be perfect? The book of Hebrews begins to tell us the answer:

> But [as it is] these sacrifices annually bring a fresh remembrance of sins [to be atoned for], because the blood of bulls and goats is powerless to take sins away. Hence, when He [Christ] entered into the world, He said, Sacrifices and offerings You have not desired, but instead You have made ready a body for Me [to offer]; in burnt offerings and sin offerings You have taken no delight. Then I said, Behold, here I am, coming to do Your will, O God—[to fulfill] what is written of Me in the volume of the Book.
>
> HEBREWS 10:3-7

Christ entered the world to buy back our perfection that was lost in the Garden. Jesus, the perfect Lamb of God, did what we cannot do. He lived a perfect life and therefore had the right to be our blood offering. He paid for our sins. Hebrews 9:22 says, "Without the shedding of blood there is no forgiveness of sins" (ESV).

In Hebrews 10:10 we read, "And in accordance with this will [of God], we have been made holy (consecrated and sanctified) through the offering made once for all." Then in verse 14 we're given the same mercy that Isaiah was given: "For by a single offering He has forever completely cleansed and perfected those who are consecrated and made holy." Don't you love the word *forever*? We are completely cleansed and perfected. Perfected . . . the price required to get into heaven. God has made us holy through the offering made once for all.

> Whereas this One [Christ], after He had offered a
> single sacrifice for our sins [that shall avail] for all time,
> sat down at the right hand of God, then to wait until
> His enemies should be made a stool beneath His feet.
> For by a single offering He has forever completely
> cleansed and perfected those who are consecrated and
> made holy.
>
> HEBREWS 10:12-14

Jesus offered one single sacrifice, forever, for all. Then He *sat down* (Jewish priests did not sit down in the Temple because their work was never done). Jesus, our High Priest, finished His work on our behalf and sat down. How was it completed? *Completely. Perfectly.* For how long? *Forever.*

When someone asks you the question, "What does God think of you?" just answer them, "He thinks I'm perfect." God sees you through Jesus-colored glasses. We now live the exchanged life. Jesus took our sin and unrighteousness, and we received His perfect record.

Isaiah had seen one more thing as he looked at God. Not only did he see himself clean and forgiven, but he also saw the needs of those around him. He said, "I dwell in the midst of a people of unclean lips; for my eyes have seen the King, the Lord of hosts!" (Isaiah 6:5). God had truly allowed him to see others through His eyes.

Oh, to see the people in my world with His eyes. God came to seek and to save that which was lost. When we truly see what God has done for us, we then can see for the first time the needs of others through the eyes of His love. This includes seeing our children.

After Isaiah had been made clean, he then was offered a call to answer. In Hebrews 6:8 it is almost as if the Godhead allows him to listen in on a conversation between Father, Son, and Holy Spirit. The Lord said, "Whom shall I send? And who will go for Us?" Isaiah had already seen his own need, a need that had been met. God then calls him to meet the needs he had seen in others. I can almost visualize Isaiah's response after he had been made clean and been forgiven. I think his response was "Here! Me! Over here! Me! Here I am. Will I do? Send me!" The Lord's answer was for him to go and tell the people.

This book does not contain any magic tricks. It has only one answer: Jesus. He alone can make us fit for heaven and fit to live a holy life here on earth. Remember, holiness is the habit of being of one mind with God, hating what He hates and loving what He loves. It also means measuring everything by His standard, God's Word. He has said to us, "You shall be holy, for I am holy" (1 Peter 1:16). This is possible only because Jesus has offered Himself for us; we now have hope for ourselves and for future generations. He is a transforming God. God's signature in our lives is a desire to be holy.

In the foreword of Nancy Leigh DeMoss's book *Holiness: The Heart God Purifies*, Randy Alcorn writes:

God is the reason we should be holy. But He's also the empowerment for our holiness. Many of us are convinced we should be more holy, but we've gone about it wrong. To be holy in our strength, and for our glory, is to be distinctly unholy. To be holy in Christ's strength and for His glory . . . that's our calling, and our joy. . . . True holiness isn't cold and deadening—it's warm and inviting. It's irresistible.[1]

Many years ago, I was mentoring three young women who drove forty-five minutes every week to meet with me. As the weeks turned into months, one of the young women said, "I finally get it. I know the answer to every question that Shelia asks us." The other two women waited to hear her answer. She said one word: "Jesus!" We all laughed and laughed. She was joking, but do you know what? She was right. Jesus is the answer to our heart's cries for ourselves, our husbands, our children, our friends, and our world. Real life comes from a yielded heart. That is our only hope, and that hope is found in the person of Jesus Christ. If our dreamers are to have truly meaningful and successful lives, they have to flow out of a yielded heart.

ESSENTIAL 5:

Fight the Dream Killers

THERE ARE THREE DREAM KILLERS that can destroy our God-given dreams and cause us to live in defeat and hopelessness. What are these dream killers? The Bible shows us: the world, the flesh, and the devil. We need to fight these dream killers and teach our children to fight them too.

To be successful in this effort, we must first learn some things about this battle into which we have been born. First of all, we need to know that this battle is in the spiritual realm. There is an unseen war going on. I remember hearing a story about natives coming to kill a missionary. When the missionary woke up the next morning, one of the native warriors came to talk with him. He told him that they had planned to kill him and his family, but they were thwarted. When they reached the hut, they saw a large army surrounding it. The missionary said that he had not seen an army that night, but the Lord had allowed the natives to see into the invisible world.

We see this in Scripture as well. In 2 Kings 6:15-23, Elisha responded to the news of the city being surrounded, replying,

"Fear not; for those with us are more than those with them" (verse 16). The young servant looked out and saw only the enemy, but Elisha saw something more. He saw the army of God. Elisha then prayed, "Lord, I pray You, open his eyes that he may see" (verse 17). See what? See the invisible world. "And the Lord opened the young man's eyes, and he saw, and behold, the mountain was full of horses and chariots of fire round about Elisha" (verse 17). Read the rest of the story, which ends with, "And the bands of Syria came no more into the land of Israel" (verse 23).

We find another man of God in the book of Daniel. Daniel had been greatly troubled and had prayed and fasted for three weeks when he said, "I lifted up my eyes and looked, and behold, a man clothed in linen, whose loins were girded with pure gold of Uphaz. His body also was [a golden luster] like beryl, his face had the appearance of lightning, his eyes were like flaming torches, his arms and his feet like glowing burnished bronze, and the sound of his words was like the noise of a multitude [of people or the roaring of the sea]" (Daniel 10:5-6). Daniel was the only one who could see this heavenly being.

> And [the angel] said to me, O Daniel, you greatly
> beloved man, understand the words that I speak to
> you and stand upright, for to you I am now sent.
> And while he was saying this word to me, I stood up
> trembling. Then he said to me, Fear not, Daniel, for
> from the first day that you set your mind and heart
> to understand and to humble yourself before your
> God, your words were heard, and I have come as a

consequence of [and in response to] your words. But the prince of the kingdom of Persia withstood me for twenty-one days. Then Michael, one of the chief [of the celestial] princes, came to help me, for I remained there with the kings of Persia.

DANIEL 10:11-13

This angel said Daniel was greatly loved, he was heard on the first day he prayed, and that the angel was there because of Daniel's prayer. If all of this were true, why did the angel not come for three weeks? He was in a battle in heavenly places, and Michael had come to help him, which allowed him to assist Daniel. I don't know about you, but this blows my mind! I do not even pretend to understand this. There exists a whole world unseen by human eyes (unless the Lord allows). How do I know this? The Bible tells us this in Ephesians 6:12: "For we are not wrestling with flesh and blood [contending only with physical opponents], but against the despotisms, against the powers, against [the master spirits who are] the world rulers of this present darkness, against the spirit forces of wickedness in the heavenly (supernatural) sphere."

The good news is the winner has already been determined because of the death and resurrection of Jesus Christ. Satan's fate has been sealed. On the cross Jesus proclaimed, "It is finished." He had paid for sin. When He arose from the grave, the final victory had been won, the victory over death.

Jesus said all authority, all power in heaven and on earth is His (see Matthew 28:18). He has won not only our salvation but also our daily victory, which produces victorious living in Christ.

The World

But to live victoriously, we need to battle the dream killers. Our first enemy is the world. The pattern of this world refers to the philosophies and systems of how people collectively choose to live on the earth. Examples are worldly mind-sets (philosophies that oppose God) that are found in how we choose to live, dress, and relate to people. Moral standards of the world are relative; right or wrong is determined by the leaders just as the length of a foot in the Middle Ages was determined by the current king's shoe size. The world can kill your dreams by changing them through compromise. Worldly attitudes and behaviors can go undetected because they are ingrained in the culture of our world.

As believers, we are not to conform to the norms of how others live but to live to please God, who is not of this world. To do that, Romans 12:2 says that we have to change the way we think. We must renew our minds:

> Do not be conformed to this world (this age), [fashioned
> after and adapted to its external, superficial customs],
> but be transformed (changed) by the [entire] renewal of
> your mind [by its new ideals and its new attitude], so
> that you may prove [for yourselves] what is the good and
> acceptable and perfect will of God, even the thing which
> is good and acceptable and perfect [in His sight for you].

We must learn to think like God thinks, and in order to do this we must know what God thinks. He has told us in the Bible how we should live.

Have you ever read *The Pilgrim's Progress?* In the book, Vanity Fair is the town that represents the world. The world lures and tempts Pilgrim, the main character. One of our family's phrases we use when we are being tempted is found in the movie *A Bug's Life*. It is "Don't look at the light." It's from the scene where the bugs begin to look at a bug zapper in the yard. The zapper pulls them in, and they get zapped. That's what the world is like. It looks so good, and before long we are zapped, stuck, and our dreams are changed or killed.

We are not to be conformed, but we are to be transformed by the Word of God because it is the Truth: "I do not ask that You will take them out of the world, but that You will keep and protect them from the evil one. They are not of the world (worldly, belonging to the world), [just] as I am not of the world. Sanctify them [purify, consecrate, separate them for Yourself, make them holy] by the Truth; Your Word is Truth" (John 17:15-17).

The Flesh

The second dream killer we must face is by far the hardest. This one is difficult because it is the monster within—ourselves! God's ways are not natural to us. I once heard Dr. Wayne Barber, a teacher with Precept Ministries, say, "The biggest enemy you will ever face looks at you in the mirror every morning."

The battle with the first dream killer, the world, is won by changing our minds through the Word of God, but the only way to gain victory over our enemy of the flesh is death to the self-life. This enemy is our flesh (our fallen nature). Our flesh never changes, and it never gets better.

We can believe that the battle in the spiritual realm is ongoing and real even though we cannot see it. We can accept the truth about how the world lures and tempts us. But we must understand that the hardest, most exhausting battle of them all takes place within our own hearts.

When we came to Christ and accepted His salvation, His Spirit came to live in us, but our old nature did not go away. The Scripture calls it the old man. This is where the battle commences. Who will govern our lives, self or Christ? There is only one answer to this problem—we must die to the self-life. The Scripture calls it death to self. The flesh must be crucified (my emphasis added here):

> Therefore consider the members of your earthly body *as dead* to immorality, impurity, passion, evil desire, and greed, which amounts to idolatry.
>
> COLOSSIANS 3:5, NASB

> Knowing this, that *our old self was crucified with Him*, in order that our body of sin might be done away with, so that we would no longer be slaves to sin; for he who has died is freed from sin. Now if *we have died with Christ*, we believe that we shall also live with Him.
>
> ROMANS 6:6-8, NASB

> Even so *consider yourselves to be dead to sin*, but alive to God in Christ Jesus. Therefore do not let sin reign in your mortal body so that you obey its lusts, and do not go on presenting the members of your body to sin as instruments of unrighteousness; but present yourselves to God as those alive from the dead, and your members as instruments of righteousness to God.
>
> ROMANS 6:11-13, NASB

We are dead to sin, but very much alive to God. Galatians 2:20 says, "I have been crucified with Christ; and it is no longer I who live, but Christ lives in me; and the life which I now live in the flesh I live by faith in the Son of God, who loved me and gave Himself up for me" (NASB). Therefore, we are to walk not according to the flesh but according to the Spirit. Being spiritually minded yields life and peace in Christ. If I want the Christ-filled life, I must choose to exchange my dead life for the living life. My feelings of unhappiness, defeat, discouragement, and despair are converted to love, joy, and peace, which are gifts provided by the Spirit. We are now free to exchange our poverty for God's wealth, our weakness for His strength.

We need to understand what it means to be dead to self. A dead man has no worries and no rights. We do not belong to ourselves any longer but to God so we can do His good pleasure. We can now make a decisive dedication to die to our ways and our wishes in order to do the wishes of our living Savior. Consider what Paul says in Romans 12:1: "I appeal to you therefore, brethren, and beg of you in view of [all] the mercies of God, to make a decisive dedication of your bodies [presenting all your members and faculties] as a living sacrifice, holy (devoted, consecrated) and well pleasing to God, which is your reasonable (rational, intelligent) service and spiritual worship."

Death means yielding my rights forever to call the shots in my own life. Now I do what God wants to do. I say what He wants to say. I go where He wants to go. My life, my body, and my mouth are not mine but His.

Have you ever understood that because you are in Christ, you were nailed to the cross, buried, and raised to newness of life and that you are *free* to walk like this is true? Have you ever made a *decisive dedication* and presented yourself to God as a living sacrifice, which is your reasonable service? If not, will you do that right now?

Once we are living this way, we are told to remind ourselves daily of the fact that we are dead to self. We are to learn to walk not after the flesh but to walk in the Spirit. You are no longer a slave, so start living like a free woman! We are free to really live, and we can teach our dream chasers to be free also.

The reason that our old nature had to die with Jesus was so that we could be free to walk in newness of life and live in the likeness of His resurrection. We are no longer slaves to sin. Our chains are gone. We should fall at His feet in gratitude.

> We were buried therefore with Him by the baptism
> into death, so that just as Christ was raised from the
> dead by the glorious [power] of the Father, so we
> too might [habitually] live and behave in newness of
> life. For if we have become one with Him by sharing
> a death like His, we shall also be [one with Him
> in sharing] His resurrection [by a new life lived for
> God]. . . . We know that our old (unrenewed) self
> was nailed to the cross with Him in order that [our]
> body [which is the instrument] of sin might be made
> ineffective and inactive for evil, that we *might no
> longer be the slaves of sin.*"]
> ROMANS 6:4-6, EMPHASIS ADDED

The result is that we are freed, loosed, and delivered from the power of sin. Death no longer has power over us. We are going to live forever and have unbroken fellowship with God.

Now that we know this, we ask, Now what? We are to consider it as truth and therefore live like it. What about sin? Basically, Jesus says *stop*. The reason He says this is because we can, by the new power that now indwells us, choose to stop sinning and start living as though we are believers who have been raised from the dead.

How does this work in my everyday life? Our old nature did not go away when Christ came in, and it's at war with us. God tells us to fight against those sinful feelings, and for the first time we are free to fight. We can live a victorious life as we learn to fight in God's power against the very nature within us.

We are to stop pleasing the world and ourselves and are to start pleasing God. One question Hank and I taught our sons to ask themselves when deciding about doing something was, *Does this please the Lord?* The world and even some of those in the church say life is about pleasing yourself. The world says that I, my family, my stuff, my happiness, my desires are all that matter, or are at least the first things that matter. That's not what the Word of God says.

In the Bible, Paul tells us to put off the old nature and put on the new man. He tells us to take off those old graveclothes, those old sin bents. We are to put on our new robes of righteousness, our new spiritual selves, which are being renewed and remolded. Remolded into what? Into the very perfect image of Jesus.

I grew up in a small town in Alabama. When I would go shopping on Main Street, I would often meet someone I did not know who would walk up to me and say, "You must be Seab Daniel's daughter. You look just like him." Is that what people think about us regarding Jesus? Do they say, "You must be a child of the King, because you look just like Him"?

The Bible compares the refinement of silver to what God does in our lives through the Holy Spirit because of our relationship with Jesus. The process to refine silver must be done right. The silver is heated and the dross or the impurities float to the top, and the silversmith scrapes them off. He then turns up the heat to bring more impurities to the top. He continues this process until all the impurities have risen and been scraped away. He must watch the silver always, for if it's heated too much it will be destroyed. Do you know when the silversmith knows the silver is refined? It's when he can see his reflection in the silver.

We are the silver, and God is the silversmith. Sometimes the process of refinement is painful, but through it all God never leaves us. Just as the silversmith knows that he must watch the silver to make sure it's not heated too much and thus injured, so God watches over the refining process until He sees His reflection in us. Malachi 3:3 says, "And he shall sit as a refiner and purifier of silver" (KJV).

Our dreamers need to have their lives refined and purified though the Holy Spirit, who indwells their spirits. He will instruct their minds, control their wills, and control their emotions and therefore change their actions. But He will only do this with their permission and never without it. This is the only way to deal with the dream killer of the flesh.

The Devil

What happens when we decide to follow the will of God? That's when the battle really begins. The battle is waged because we are given the power to overcome sin's grip. There is no battle when there's no opposing side. It takes two to fight. When you became one with Christ, His enemy became your enemy as well.

Who is God's enemy and our ancient foe? He's the king of this world, and he controls all of this world. He is Satan. It is he who offered Jesus the kingdoms of the world when He was going through temptation in the wilderness.

Satan is a created being and is the wisest and most beautiful creature God ever made. He's not the horned creature of Greek mythology or the cartoon character with a red suit, a tail, horns, and a pitchfork. In Scripture, we see him being described as deceptively beautiful. If we could see him, we would think he's the most beautiful creature we have ever seen. (In 2 Corinthians 11:14, Paul says Satan transformed himself into an angel of light.)

Sometime after his creation, but before God created man, Satan became prideful and rebelled against God. In his rebellion, he convinced one-third of the angels to side with him and led them into rebellion. These angels were cast out with him by God and are now referred to as demons. Michael, an archangel of God, fought with God's angels against Satan and his angels (demons). Satan lost the battle and was cast from heaven down to earth. This was the first battle in this ongoing war between God and Satan.

After creation, because he hates God, Satan convinced Eve that God had lied to her. Satan led her into rebellion and continues in his rebellion today.

The Bible says that Satan will continue in his rebellion against God until the very end. Someday God is going to get rid of him for good, but for now he is God's enemy, and because we (born-again ones) belong to God, Satan is our enemy as well.

That enemy does everything he can to keep us from the truth of the Cross. Once we accept the truth of the Cross and enter into God's family, he continues to try and keep us from the victory that is our birthright. He does not want us to see the truth that sets us free, truth that causes us to no longer be victims but victors.

As Genesis 3:1 tells us, Satan is subtle and crafty. He takes truth and presents it to us with just a little twist so it is difficult to detect. He uses indirect and deceitful methods. As an example here, I have a friend who used to work in a bank. She told me that the way they learned to detect counterfeit money was not by studying the fake money but by studying and handling the real thing, so that when there was a fake bill they knew it right away. We believers have to be so familiar with God's truth found in the Word of God that when we hear error we know it right away, as Jesus says in John 10:27: "My sheep hear my voice, and I know them, and they follow me" (ESV).

One thing I taught my sons was to hear my voice. About four years ago while they were filming the *Woodlawn* movie, we were helping entertain pastors from all over the US who were on set. One night at dinner Jon needed to get to another meeting. But he kept talking as his assistant tried to get his attention so they wouldn't be late. Jon just kept on talking. I looked at the assistant and asked, "Do you need Jon right now?" He said yes, so I quietly said, "Jon." Jon turned around and said, "Yes, do you need something?" (I'm sure that he was totally unaware of the way he responded.) As they left, his assistant said, "I need to record your voice because he hears you over the crowd." That time Jon only needed to make it to a meeting on time, but as a child there were times when listening to my voice saved his life. When the world, our flesh, and Satan scream at us so loud we cannot even think straight, we need to hear the voice of the Lord, just as Jon heard my voice that day—because our lives might depend on it.

John 18:37 reminds us to listen to Jesus and the truth: "I have come into the world, to bear witness to the Truth. Everyone who is of the Truth [who is a friend of the Truth, who belongs to the Truth] hears and listens to My voice." Jesus and His Word are the unchangeable, absolute truth. On the other hand, Satan is a liar. He leads people into rebellion by telling them lies because he hates them and wants to enslave them in sin. He can only tempt and try to persuade us to sin. He cannot force anyone to sin—especially not believers.

According to Matthew 4:1-10, when Jesus was tempted by Satan, He cited Scripture to him. So how do we combat the lies of Satan? We likewise use the truth found in the Word.

> But He gives us more and more grace (power of the Holy Spirit, to meet this evil tendency and all others fully). That is why He says, God sets Himself against the proud and haughty, but gives grace [continually] to the lowly (those who are humble enough to receive it). So be subject to God. Resist the devil [stand firm against him], and he will flee from you.
>
> JAMES 4:6-7

I love the scene in the film *War Room* when leading lady Elizabeth comes out of her war-room prayer closet, tired of the enemy making headway in her family, and she finally understands who she is in Christ. She comes out as a fearless princess warrior ready to take a stand for her family. She says aloud as she walks out the back door of her house:

> Devil, I know you can hear me. You have played with my mind and had your way long enough! No more! You are done! Jesus is the Lord of this house, and that means there's no place for you here anymore! So take your lies, your schemes, and your accusations and get out in Jesus' name! You can't have my marriage, you can't have my daughter, and you sure can't have my man! This house is under new management and that means you are out! And another thing, I am so sick of you stealing my joy, but that's changing too. My joy doesn't come from my friends, it doesn't come from my job, it doesn't even come from my husband. My joy is found in Jesus.[1]

That's the mind-set we need in order to fight our battle against Satan. Teaching your children early on to battle the evil one will keep them on their path to discovering their God-given talents.

It's clear that we have three enemies, but God has told us in the Bible what we should do about each one. We are not to be conformed to the world; we are to substitute His Spirit for our flesh, and then we are to submit to God and resist the devil. As you are training your creative children, you can show them how to avoid these dream killers.

ESSENTIAL 6:

Find Power for Living

OUR GREATEST NEED after we've become a Christian is to actually *be* the Christian we have become. We need to learn to behave as the restored creations that we are. We must teach our dreamers to live lives that follow God's calling and dreams.

How do we do that? The Bible tells us that God is the only source and power we need to live our new lives in Christ.

So how do you receive power for living? First, know that there are really only two kinds of people in the world: the person who has not received Christ's gift of salvation and the person who has accepted God's wonderful gift of salvation. The Bible identifies them as natural people (unbelievers) and spiritual people (believers). Believers in Christ are then divided into two categories as well. The Bible calls them *spiritual* and *carnal.*

> However, brethren, I could not talk to you as to
> spiritual [men], but as to nonspiritual [men of the
> flesh, in whom the carnal nature predominates], as to
> mere infants [in the new life] in Christ [unable to talk

yet!] I fed you with milk, not solid food, for you were
not yet strong enough [to be ready for it]; but even yet
you are not strong enough [to be ready for it], for you
are still [unspiritual, having the nature] of the flesh
[under the control of ordinary impulses].

1 CORINTHIANS 3:1-3

The good news is that as a child of God who trusts in Jesus'
work done on the cross, you will never be a part of the natural
(lost) person category ever again. At the moment of salvation,
God gave you His Holy Spirit, and His Spirit birthed you and
made you who were once dead spiritually alive forevermore. He
actually indwells every believer.

The Spiritual Christian

The spiritual Christian is one who has yielded her life to the
lordship of Christ, is empowered by the Holy Spirit, and is
moment by moment led and directed by Him. Wow—yielded,
empowered, and led. This kind of life is that abundant life that
Jesus came into the world to give any and all who will believe
in Him.

Jesus told us that if we abide in Him and He abides in us,
we will be Christians who will bear much fruit. As we walk
with the Lord, His presence within us begins to change us.
The longer we walk yielded to the lordship of Christ, the more
we will begin to see the fruit of the Holy Spirit in our lives:
"The fruit of the Spirit is love, joy, peace, longsuffering, kindness, goodness, faithfulness, meekness, self-control" (Galatians
5:22-23, ASV).

The Bible will teach us to believe in Him, and then we will

begin to learn to cleave to, trust in, and rely on Him. We will become more and more fruitful in abundance until our fruitfulness will begin to overflow into the lives of others, as Jesus said: "He who believes in Me, as the Scripture said, 'From his innermost being will flow rivers of living water'" (John 7:38, NASB). He said *living water*! He wants to fill us up so full that He will begin to flow from us into the lives of others and they can drink from our overflow, our river.

How many overflowing Christians have you met lately? A better question is, Are you an overflowing river? If not, do you want to be a river? If we want to be that flowing river, we must learn to trust the Bible and its author (God) with every part of our lives. There's a man mentioned in the Bible who expresses my heart concerning trust. In Mark 9:24, he said, "I believe; help my unbelief!" (ESV).

In my life at least, sometimes it seems easy to believe God, and then on another day I have to ask for help with my unbelief. It takes a lifetime to learn to trust Him, but it starts with simply saying, "I believe." There is room for doubt in the midst of faith; doubt is the shadow of faith. Without doubt, life takes no faith. Sometimes we have to work to believe.

I remember Hank telling our Andy not to run from his doubt but to run toward his doubt. Take your questions to Jesus because He has the answers. Thomas was not with the other disciples when Jesus appeared to them after being resurrected, and he too expressed doubt, but Jesus met him with the answer he needed in John 20:27: "Then saith he to Thomas, Reach hither thy finger, and behold my hands; and reach hither thy hand, and thrust it into my side: and be not faithless, but believing" (KJV).

Some of you may feel that life has taught you not to trust anyone. Or maybe the pain of life has caused you to live in your frustration, exasperation, disappointment, anger, and fear. I want you to know that life is not fair and we live in a very broken, sinful world. In fact, we ourselves were broken before we came to Christ.

God knows where you are in your walk and will always meet you where you are in ways you can grasp. Right now, will you stop and ask Him for help? You can go to Him with all your questions, tell Him how you really feel, and lay it all out before Him in prayer.

The Carnal Christian

The second type of Christian is the carnal Christian. This person has also received Christ as her Savior but lives in defeat because she is trying to live the Christian life by her own strength. This was how I lived from the time I was a six-year-old to the time I was twenty. I am so deeply grateful that I was introduced to the Lord Jesus as my Redeemer at such a young age, but the one thing that was not made adequately clear to me (I do not know if it was not taught in my church or if it was and I did not understand it) was that not only had Christ died for me; He also rose again to live through me. Knowing Him experientially only as the way to heaven, it took me many weary and defeated years to come to know Him as my life. Carnal Christians are true believers, but they are living according to the flesh and therefore are not experiencing an abundant or fruitful life.

There are many different ways people refer to the carnal Christian—the flesh, the old nature, the old man—but whatever you call it, the carnal Christian is under the control of ordinary human impulses. We were born with our old nature, and it continued to develop as we learned to meet our own needs, protect our emotions, deal with fear and anger, shield ourselves from hurt, and live in this broken world out of our own human resources. You might hear this referred to in the world as using "coping mechanisms." In other words, it means learning to do life without recognizing a need for God.

We all have different personalities, backgrounds, achievements, hurts, and experiences, so our flesh operates in different manners. At salvation, we receive a new nature, where the Holy Spirit comes to dwell in our hearts. Yet our flesh is still there, and it never gets better.

As a Bible teacher for more than forty-five years, I've often wondered how there could be a room filled with women hearing the truth of the Word taught, all hearing the same thing yet not all going away with the same life change. I have come to understand that we all have filters in our brains and our souls that have been established by the world, the flesh, and Satan. If we are still controlled by the flesh, we even filter the Word of God incorrectly in our thinking. Instead of being focused on Jesus, everything is still all about us and how everything can benefit us. Our eyes are focused on ourselves and our needs being met. If we filter the Word of God through the flesh, we can come away with a "works" mentality. We do not understand that the Holy Spirit who saves us also wants to give us His power to live this new life in Christ; therefore we continue to strive and struggle to live by our own effort.

The Holy Spirit is to be our teacher and our new filter for thinking. When He is our teacher, we will be able to hear and apply the truth of God's Word the way He intended; otherwise our flesh will rob us of the wonder of His Word and acceptance of His grace.

The carnal person has no power to live out her new life in Christ because the flesh is powerless, even when she does good things in hopes that she will somehow change on the inside. That simply does not work. At the end of the day we are still the same, naturally bent to focus more on the outward manifestations of human good. I do not know what your flesh is like. I do not know if you are a law keeper (a Goody Two-shoes), a lawbreaker, or somewhere in between. You need to understand that these mind-sets are both carnal, and to God, flesh is flesh.

Walking in the Spirit

Unlike our salvation, the Spirit-filled life is not permanent, and we must learn to live controlled by the Spirit moment by moment. At any given instant, you are functioning either spiritually or carnally. And of course, God desires us to live out our new life in the Spirit, not in the flesh. If we are ever going to learn to be overflowing rivers, we must learn to walk being led by the Spirit and to live our lives in the Spirit.

Moms, picture in your mind the time when your children were just learning to walk. Maybe that was a long time ago, or maybe that was today. But no child just wakes up one morning and goes running around the block. They all have to first learn to stand. Then they learn to walk along the edge of the sofa, holding on for dear life. Then comes that first step without holding on to anything. What if one of the times they fell, they looked up at you and said, "That's it! I knew I would never learn to walk," and never tried again? Learning to walk in the Spirit is a lot like our toddlers learning to walk. It is progressive.

Keep getting back up and try again. That is why God gave us 1 John 1:9: "If we [freely] admit that we have sinned and confess our sins, He is faithful and just (true to His own nature and promises) and will forgive our sins [dismiss our lawlessness] and [continuously] cleanse us from all unrighteousness [everything not in conformity to His will in purpose, thought, and action]."

Life is forever changing, and so are we. We must continue to learn to walk out our faith in every new season. We will never arrive. We will always be in process.

It's so important for us to learn to walk controlled by the Spirit and to obey Jesus' instructions the same way He obeyed His Father's instructions. The reason is He wants us to know His joy, and that our joy and gladness might be full as a river, overflowing out of our hearts.

There are two gardens in Scripture that affect us. The Garden of Eden was a place of defeat, a paradise lost, and it is our human inheritance. The garden of Gethsemane was a place of victory. Mankind has lived in a world damaged by the events that took place in the Garden of Eden, but thank God, we were given a second chance in the garden of Gethsemane. Jesus Christ said yes to the cross when He cried, "My Father, if it is possible, let this cup pass away from Me; nevertheless, not what I will [not what I desire], but as You will and desire" (Matthew 26:39). He won our victory, defeating sin and death and offering new life to every man, woman, and child on earth. In Matthew 16:24, Christ tells His followers that they must take up their cross and follow Him. This is a call to absolute surrender—a garden of Gethsemane experience for those who wish to be His followers. If we are to be true followers of Christ and live in the victory paid for by Christ, we must surrender our will to the will of the Father. We, too, must say "nevertheless" to God just as Christ did in the garden of Gethsemane. What follows that statement is "Not my will but Thy will be done."

Have you honestly said to God in surrender, "Not my will but Thy will be done," or as my grandson says, "He gets to be the boss of my life"?

The Spirit-filled life is a life yielded to Christ. It means we are willing to allow Him to direct our entire lives. We have to come to a place of total surrender to the lordship of Christ. This is the way Christ lives His life in and through us by the power of the Holy Spirit. When we are filled with the Holy Spirit, our lives will glorify Christ. The Holy Spirit is also the power that Christ promised just before His ascension, in Acts 1:1-9.

When Jon was young, after he had become a Christ follower, Hank and I began to teach him about the role of the Holy Spirit in his life. He was having a difficult time understanding how God through the Spirit could empower him to live the Christian life. So one morning I got up early and went to the living room and laid a glove on the floor, and about three feet away from it, I placed a book on the floor. When Jon woke up, I called him into the living room and asked, "Jon, can you think of a way that the glove can pick up the book?" He looked at me as if I had three heads. I just looked back at him and said, "There's a way. Just think about it." After a few minutes, he got it. He ran over to the glove, picked it up, put it on his hand, then picked up the book and brought it over to me. I said, "Now, that's what God does through His Spirit. The glove looks the same, but your hand is what is powering the glove, just as the power to live the Christian life is in the Spirit."

After that I took it further. "What if before you got in here this morning I went to the yard and filled the glove with dirt, and then I asked you to pick up the book with the glove? Could you do it? You would first have to get the dirt out of the glove in order to put your hand in it and pick up the book. The dirt represents sin in your life that you haven't confessed. The Lord can only fill what is empty."

Sin breaks our fellowship with God. Our first response to sin in our lives is to hide, as Adam and Eve did in the Garden after they ate the apple (see Genesis 3:8-9). Our relationship as God's child is not broken, but our fellowship with Him is interrupted. God does not break that fellowship, but instead we break it because of our sin, our guilt, and our shame. It's wonderful that God's fellowship with us is so important to Him that He comes after us asking, "Where are you?" as He did with Adam and Eve. That question comes in the form of our conviction, that uncomfortable feeling in our soul.

If you know that sin breaks fellowship with God, why would you choose to remain in your sin? You see, we are just a heartbeat, just one sin away from carnality at any given moment. Our transition into the family of God is permanent, and we will never go back to the natural man again. Yet the transition from the carnal to the spiritual is not permanent. So what are we to do? The Christian organization Cru calls this spiritual breathing:

By faith you can continue to experience God's love and forgiveness.

If you become aware of an area of your life (an attitude or an action) that is displeasing to the Lord, even though you are walking with Him and sincerely desiring to serve Him, simply thank God that He has forgiven your sins—past, present, and future—on the basis of Christ's death on the cross. Claim His love and forgiveness by faith and continue to have fellowship with Him.

If you retake the throne of your life through sin—a definite act of disobedience—breathe spiritually.

Spiritual breathing (exhaling the impure and inhaling the pure) is an exercise in faith that enables you to continue to experience God's love and forgiveness.

1. **Exhale**—confess your sin—agree with God concerning your sin and thank Him for His forgiveness of it, according to 1 John 1:9 and Hebrews 10:1-25. Confession involves repentance—a change in attitude and action.

2. **Inhale**—surrender the control of your life to Christ, and appropriate (receive) the fullness of the Holy Spirit by faith. Trust that He now directs and empowers you; according to the command of Ephesians 5:18, and the promise of 1 John 5:14, 15.[1]

When I think about the transforming power of Christ, I stand in amazement that as I have kept my eyes on Him, He has changed me. I am not that child, teenager, young adult, young wife, or new mother that I once was, and I am not yet what I will become.

Remember that one offering cleansed and perfected us in God's eyes and made us holy. What an unbelievable agreement is found in Hebrews 10:16, when God says, "I will imprint

My laws upon their hearts, and I will inscribe them on their minds (on their inmost thoughts and understanding)." This is how God puts His Holy Spirit in a person. Because of this we can progressively become who we are, and someday, this will be complete in our experience as well. God gave us a new heart and mind by imprinting His ways in our hearts. He gave us the Spirit and the Word to teach us to walk a new way—His way. We will be like Him.

Do not become discouraged if you are not as fruitful as someone who has known and experienced walking controlled by the Spirit for a longer time than you. As we always said in the Erwin household, "We are all in process." You will begin to grow in grace. Your study of God's Word, as well as your prayer life, will become more meaningful as you are more and more transformed into the image of Christ. You *will* begin to change. He promises it.

Just as He has promised to give you the power to be a mom to your dreamer, He will also give power to your dreamers as they yield their lives to Him.

ESSENTIAL 7:

Don't Do It Alone

RAISING UP DREAMERS and helping your children find and grow their God-given talents is not something God ever intended you to do alone. In Titus 2:3-5, the Bible instructs the older women to teach the young women and to become spiritual moms. If you do not have a spiritual mom or mentor, begin to pray that God would lead you to just the right woman to help you grow. I pray you find an older woman to encourage you in your walk with the Lord.

You also need to find a biblically sound, multigenerational women's Bible study. As the husband of a woman in my Bible study always used to say to her, "Go be with your own kind." We women need one another, and we all need to study God's Word together.

Do you have Christ-centered friends? There are levels of friendship, but you need one or two friends you can call your companions and familiar friends. You need to find wise women to do life with, those who can and will keep you on the path of righteousness, because we are told if we walk with the wise, we will become wise.

> But it was you, a man [woman (my addition here)] my equal, my companion and my familiar friend. We had sweet fellowship together and used to walk to the house of God in company.
>
> PSALM 55:13-14

> He who walks [as a companion] with wise men is wise, but he who associates with [self-confident] fools is [a fool himself and] shall smart for it.
>
> PROVERBS 13:20

I've had many dear friends over the years, but there is one friend whom I have done life with as a mother. We prayed with and for each other. We also prayed for each other's children. We have been there to encourage each other for more than twenty-six years, and now we pray for our grown children and grandchildren.

You need to make time for all of these relationships: a spiritual older woman to teach you, a good Bible study group, and a kindred-spirit friend or two. Believe me, you will be the better for it, and so will your children. Proverbs 27:17 tells us that "Iron sharpens iron; so a man sharpens the countenance of his friend."

PART FOUR

Tools

*Give your children the tools they
need for dream chasing.*

TOOL 1:

Submit to Authority

AUTHORITY IS NOT A POPULAR WORD in our society, but it is a significant word to know and understand as Christians. Hank and I sought to teach our children to live a life yielded to Christ as Lord—therefore also yielded to those God has put as authorities over them.

I told them that if they ever wanted to be effective leaders, they had to learn to be under authority. I remember hearing the late pastor Adrian Rogers unfalteringly say, "You can't be over until you are under."

Yielding to authority is one of the most important attitudes of the Christian life and of effective dream chasing. If we are not yielded and obedient, we are not walking in the Spirit, and we have no power to live the Christian life. It's possible to have knowledge of God, to go through the motions of worshiping Him, and even to have wonderful religious experiences, but if there is no evidence of a yielded, obedient heart, God says it's only good works, which, by the way, Isaiah 64:6 says are "filthy rags" in God's sight. Remember, obedience is better than sacrifice. Jesus said, "If you love me, you will keep my commandments" (John 14:15, ESV).

We then sought to live before God in obedience to Him. I was always aware of the importance of my walk with the Lord and did not want to be a stumbling block for our sons. So much of what a child learns is through observation. No wonder Christ said it's better to have a millstone hung around your neck and be thrown into the sea than cause one of His little ones to stumble. When God gifts us a little one, it must be a priority for us to walk closely with Him.

Hank and I have not lived perfect lives, but we have sought to live blameless lives. After Andy and Jon joined our family, I wanted twice as much to be that river of living water that God promised would flow out of my innermost being. I wanted my sons to know without a shadow of a doubt that God is worth obeying.

One night when the boys were in their early teens, before Andy was driving, Hank and I were catching a ride into town with another couple for a Bible study. We lived in no-man's-land, and at the time, no one would deliver pizzas that far out. The boys requested that the friends picking us up would bring them a pizza and were really counting on it. A miscommunication happened, though, and the couple arrived—with no pizza. I saw my sons' faces fall. I lifted up my hand in a "stop" position, as was our custom, and said, "Yield." I smiled and they smiled back as we left. After I got to the Bible study, I called home to see how they were doing. Happy voices greeted me with a story of making pizza out of bagels. This was a worth-it moment, and I was thrilled as a parent over their yielded spirits.

Another time, Andy was invited at the last minute to go to El

Salvador on a mission trip. He and his father had talked about it, and he had also sought outside counsel. Then it occurred to him that he had not checked in with me, his mother, to get my "heartbeat" on the matter. I was fine with him going. I trusted my husband's decision, and if I had felt otherwise I would have told him. Andy asked me if I had peace about him going on the trip. He then asked me if I would pray about it. If the Lord did not give me peace, he said he would not go. He felt he had to have all green lights to go. I took the decision at hand to the Lord that night. When the morning came, I called Andy into my room to let him know that I had perfect peace about him going on the trip. His reply was, "Yes!" He fell to his knees and said, "I wanted to go so bad."

Yielded, he was willing to go and willing to stay—always willing to obey. Remember what Jesus said in Luke 22:42: "Not my will, but yours, be done" (ESV).

TOOL 2:

Dare Them to Be a Daniel

FIRST OF ALL, not all peer pressure is bad. Some peer pressure can be good. Group encouragement in the ways of the Lord is beneficial. But what do we do if peer pressure is negative and detrimental? To find and develop God-given dreams and talents, children will need to learn to be their own person and resist negative peer pressure. If your dreamers are to be leaders in the pursuit of the call, they must learn to stand alone.

We started teaching our children when they were very young to stand alone. We told them, "Others may, but we do not." One of the major lessons we taught them is found in the life of a young man by the name of Daniel.

> And the [Babylonian] king told Ashpenaz, the master of his eunuchs, to bring in some of the children of Israel, both of the royal family and of the nobility—youths without blemish, well-favored in appearance and skillful in all wisdom, discernment, and understanding, apt in learning knowledge, competent

to stand and serve in the king's palace—and to teach
them the literature and language of the Chaldeans.

DANIEL 1:3-4

Who was this group of young men? They were Jewish roy-
alty and nobility. They were the best-looking kids in Israel. They
were wise, discerning, and had understanding. They were smart!
They were competent. Wow—these were the best that Israel
had to offer, the best of the best. We do not know how many
there were, but we do know the names of four of the children
of Judah: Daniel, Hananiah, Mishael, and Azariah. We all know
the name Daniel, but the other three you might know better by
the names they were given in Babylon. These three young men
were called Shadrach, Meshach, and Abednego. God had plans
for all four of these young men.

And the king assigned for them a daily portion of his
own rich and dainty food and of the wine which he
drank. They were to be so educated and so nourished
for three years that at the end of that time they might
stand before the king.

DANIEL 1:5

We taught our sons that there was a large group, and then
there were four. Daniel was the leader of the four.

But Daniel determined in his heart that he would
not defile himself by [eating his portion of] the king's
rich and dainty food or by [drinking] the wine which
he drank; therefore he requested of the chief of the

eunuchs that he might [be allowed] not to defile himself.

DANIEL 1:8

Then there was *one*, Daniel, who made a heart decision. He was determined (he made up his mind) that he would do the right thing. That little Jewish boy knew that the king's food was not lawful food for him to eat. He chose not to eat the food provided. It was clear that he was a young man of character. Far away from home, it would have been so easy to just go with the crowd. He did not demand or argue with the man in charge; he requested politely. He requested that he be allowed not to defile himself and instead to eat only vegetables and water instead of the king's rich food.

But the chief was afraid for his own head, so Daniel and his three friends asked that they be allowed to eat the vegetables for ten days as a test. At the end of those ten days, they were in better physical shape than all the other young men who ate from the king's table. Then the steward gave everybody the same diet Daniel had been eating.

What was the result? God rewarded them. He gave them knowledge and skill and wisdom. To Daniel he gave understanding of all kinds as well as visions and dreams. When they all went before the king to converse with him, he observed no one was found like Daniel and his three friends. In fact, he found them far superior to all the other young men (see Daniel 1:17-20).

Daniel purposed in his heart not to defile himself, and therefore he acted in a certain way. One key thing to notice is that he determined what to do before he asked. It's vital that our children make that commitment before they go out with friends. If your purpose is not already decided in your heart before the temptation comes, you might make the wrong decision when you are under pressure.

When I was in my early teens, my youth leader did a project with us. He had us list what we would determine *not* to do. I made my list and taped it on my mirror. Each morning I looked at that list and was reminded of my commitment to the Lord. Therefore, when many things came up in my life, the decision was already made. I just had to walk in it.

One of the keys to overcoming peer pressure is that the heart must be fully committed to Jesus and His lordship. We taught Andy and Jon that God sees them even when no one else does. Even when we're not with them, the Lord is always there, and their goal is to please God with their actions.

We started early to build strong family ties, to develop good communication with our boys, to make them feel important, to make sure we spent time together and that they understood that we enjoy being with them. Laughter is good medicine. We made this a theme in our home. Life together is fun. Hank and I enjoy one another's fellowship and have taught them to enjoy that same fellowship with us and with each other. Then we started to include their friends in our family.

Hank was so good to take time to play with our sons. In fact, some of the kids in the neighborhood would come to the front door and ask if Mr. Erwin could come out to play with them.

We also tried to make home a safe place where love was the theme. We acted in love in our relationship with each other and helped our children become each other's best friends. When a good base was established, we brought friends into our home. We provided friends of all ages, not just friends their own age.

Hank and I worked with teenagers for more than twenty years. The one thing that we observed the most with those teens was that their moms and dads had their lives and the teens had their lives, and because they longed for a place where they felt accepted, they turned to their peers. They would do anything to be accepted by their peer group. They had become peer-dependent. They just wanted a place where they felt loved, needed, important, and accepted. We as parents have to work hard to make sure that place of safety for our children is in our own home.

Hank taught them that they must combat negative peer pressure with positive peer pressure. They are to be the ones to set the standard, not the ones who follow the bad standard. Our boys had the advantage of having a father who was a man of integrity and who has always been willing to stand alone. Likewise, I have heard Andy tell young actors to determine in their hearts what they will and will not do in order to be a success with their craft. The day they are offered a job is not the time to make that decision.

TOOL 3:

Cultivate Good Attitudes

ATTITUDE IS SO VERY IMPORTANT if your dreamer is to be successful in their life calling. The concept of attitude is all throughout Scripture, as it deals with a person's whole perspective on life. Basically, attitude is an entire viewpoint on life. It's expressed in a disposition and a series of emotions that reveal our beliefs about God and life in general.

A good attitude is essentially looking at life from God's perspective. God has given us the formula for a good attitude in life. I do not produce it; He produces it! All I have to do is yield control of my life on a moment-by-moment basis to the power of the indwelling Holy Spirit, who can produce all the qualities I long to experience.

Because Jesus Christ is our standard, I looked in the Word to see what kinds of attitudes He displayed. They were love, kindness, servanthood, obedience, submissiveness, joyfulness, gratefulness, meekness, and humility. When children and adults alike understand these attributes of God, we begin to want them in our lives too.

I believe that one of the major problems in America today is a lack of gratefulness. It seems as if many Americans have grown to believe they deserve to have the best of everything, to receive everything they want, and to have it when they want it. In a nation of excess, how do we cultivate gratefulness in our children? Personally, I found I first had to make sure I cultivated gratefulness in myself. I had to acknowledge and address the areas in my life where I had been ungrateful. My Bible teacher reminded me often that if I got what I truly deserved (as a sinner), it would be to burn in hell forever, but because of what Jesus did for me, I am not going to burn in hell forever. Anything short of that is a blessing!

Since we moms are the heartbeat of our families, we must guard our hearts and make sure we teach our children that every difficulty is an opportunity to see God work. Do you see opportunities embedded within your difficulties?

We tried to teach our children that when they have a need or want, they are to always pray first, even if they have the money for it, to make sure that God wants them to spend the money that way.

Let me tell you a funny story about Jon. When we started teaching our boys about giving back to God, we began with a tithe of 10 percent. When they would get money, 10 percent went in their tithe sock, 20 percent into savings, and then they could spend the rest. When the tithe sock got full, we would let them give to one of our church's missionaries. After they started to learn the joy of giving to God's work, we then taught them that it all belonged to God. He had the right to direct them with how they spent their money.

Jon was about eight years old when this concept was first

introduced to him. The look on his face was so funny as he asked in a loud, sad voice, "You mean I never get any money of my own again?" We quickly explained it to him again, and he understood that indeed he would get to spend the money; he just had to check with Jesus first. Jesus is the boss of even our money.

I agree with my friend Bruce Peters, director of communications at World Reach, Inc., who said, "God has taught me that *gratitude* is both the *means* and *measure* of spiritual maturity. Nor is *gratitude* happenstance: Indeed, believers should be intentional and diligent in the pursuit and maintenance of a grateful heart. Cultivate it by the work of the Spirit. Expect it—don't just hope for it. And I think *gratitude* is an antidote for life's ills and heavy hearts."

TOOL 4:

Keep a Clean Heart

PROVERBS 4:23 SAYS, "Keep your heart with all vigilance, for from it flow the springs of life" (ESV). As parents, our first job is to introduce each of our children to the Lord Jesus Christ. His blood will cleanse their hearts and begin to change them from the inside out. Once they make their decision for Christ, parents need to teach their children how to keep their hearts clean, because without clean hearts they are powerless and will live defeated Christian lives. Here again, you are the teacher, but they have to have their own relationship with Christ.

What are some of the things that we tried to teach our children about this truth? That's a hard question because it involves a lifetime of teaching, yet several essentials come to mind. First we taught them to understand what sin was and that they were sinners. From birth, we tried to call sin *sin*. We did not call it their disobedience, bad choices, mistakes, or anything other than sin. We started when they were young to make sure they understood that when they sinned, it was against God and not us.

We also introduced the gospel and the need for a Savior from the beginning. I understood that my first job as a parent was to get them to the Cross. I wanted them to understand that no matter how good they were, we would always fall short of God's goodness and that Jesus was their only hope. Only Jesus can take care of their sin problems and give them clean hearts.

Once they came to Christ on their own and put their trust in Him, then the work began to teach them how to work out their own salvation (see Philippians 2:12). That does not mean that they had to do good works to keep it or to prove that they have put their trust in Jesus. It meant they had to work to believe that Jesus provides all we need to live a life of holiness, and that they must learn to walk in His provision.

We taught them 1 John 1:9: "If we [freely] admit that we have sinned and confess our sins, He is faithful and just [true to His own nature and promises], and will forgive our sins and cleanse us continually from all unrighteousness" (AMP). We wanted them to understand that they have no power of their own to live the Christian life. The only way to live the Christian life is to stay clean by confession of their sin to Him and to yield their life to His control. Jesus was and is the only one who can produce His life in and through them, and He uses only clean vessels.

We tried to explain to them that the Christian life is one of obedience and submission to Jesus and that as believers, they would yield and obey. If not, they must confess and then yield and obey. The rest is up to Him. We tried to give them all the tools they would need to live a life of victory but knew we could not do it for them. They had to go to Jesus for themselves.

TOOL 5:

Deal with Conflict

IN ORDER TO BE SUCCESSFUL with anything in life, you will have to deal with conflict! How did we deal with conflict in our home? We just never disagreed! You know that's not true. When Hank was at Dallas Theological Seminary, Howard Hendricks, a professor there, told us that if a husband and wife always agree about everything, then one of them is unnecessary. We need each other's input into our lives, and over the past forty-seven years, we have learned to communicate in a manner that honors the Lord.

We must learn to appreciate one another's differences. As Hank always used to say, "Never let the devil get the victory." We have learned to talk it out, even if it takes all night! No arguing! That means no name-calling or belittling one another. If you can't resolve it, find someone you both trust to help you.

Hank and I learned early on that teasing could do great harm to a relationship. Hank says, "Teasing is a joke with some truth and a slap at the end." So we don't tease each other, and we then tried to teach our sons not to tease each other.

As parents, we tried hard to keep the lines of communication open with our sons as well. Open communication is so very important in our relationships. We must get to know our children if we're to communicate with them and help them find and develop their God-given talents and dreams. We need to know what makes them happy, sad, joyful, angry, fearful, and so on. The only way I know that we can get to know them is to spend time with them: lots and lots of time. We need to see them as our greatest ministry, our personal disciples. We should aspire to teach them the ways of the Lord and to be there for them, not only to talk to them, but to listen to them as well.

As I raised my children, I asked the Lord to teach me how to see them as He saw them. Because I wanted to help Andy and Jon know themselves and to understand just how Jesus saw them, I made sure they felt that they were and still are special to me and to the Lord. I wanted them to feel that they were safe with me and to believe that whatever bothered them was important to me, no matter how small it may have seemed.

I prayed that they might know that I wanted to see them learning to walk with Jesus and that I was there for them to help them do just that. I wanted them to know that they could share their hearts with their dad and me. Together, we would find victory in God.

Real communication has to start at a young age. We parents have to work at keeping the door open. Once the door is closed, reopening it is difficult.

One of the things we did to help them have a voice with us and yet learn to be respectful was to use the phrase explained earlier in this book: "May I please speak?" We then taught our sons to honor one another and to love each other. They also had to learn to appreciate each other's differences, given that they are very different in personality and have diverse interests. They also have distinct spiritual gifts. I taught them about the various personality types, and we also did a study on spiritual gifts. This helped them understand that there is not just one way to think and do things.

Just as Hank and I did not yell, scream, hit, or call each other names, we did not allow our sons to yell, scream, hit, or call each other names. We taught them that if you have a problem, you talk it out. If you cannot talk it out, you go to someone who can help you talk it out. If there was ever an argument, we disciplined both sons. It takes two people to have a conflict. You can always walk away.

Since Jesus is our standard, let's look at how He responded to conflict:

> For even to this were you called [it is inseparable from your vocation]. For Christ also suffered for you, leaving you [His personal] example, so that you should follow in His footsteps. He was guilty of no sin, neither was deceit (guile) ever found on His lips. When He was reviled and insulted, He did not revile or offer insult in return; [when] He was abused and suffered, He made no threats [of vengeance]; but he trusted [Himself and everything] to Him Who judges fairly.
>
> I PETER 2:21-23

When you read these Bible verses, you may think, *There's no way I can be like Jesus when it comes to conflict!* I love something our pastor mentioned the other day as he was speaking about that very concept. As he was telling us about our struggle with sin, he said, "You do understand that it's not okay for you to stay like that." Remember, we have a transforming God.

How did Christ accomplish loving others? He was reviled and insulted. He was guilty of no sin. His response was not to open His mouth. How did He do that? He trusted Himself and everything to God, His Father who judges fairly. If you will allow Jesus to do so, He will teach you how to live a new way.

First, we need to realize that quarrels come from within us, as James 4:1-3 explains.

> What leads to strife (discord and feuds) and how do conflicts (quarrels and fightings) originate among you? Do they not arise from your sensual desires that are ever warring in your bodily members? You are jealous and covet [what others have] and your desires go unfulfilled; [so] you become murderers. [To hate is to murder as far as your hearts are concerned.] You burn with envy and anger and are not able to obtain [the gratification, the contentment, and the happiness that you seek], so you fight and war. You do not have, because you do not ask. [Or] you do ask [God for them] and yet fail to receive, because you ask with wrong purpose and evil, selfish motives. Your intention is [when you get what you desire] to spend it in sensual pleasures.

So now we are back to our hearts—we are jealous and covet, which leads to envy and anger. I love that the Lord reminds us that the reason we do not have is because we do not ask, or we do ask and do not receive because of wrong motives. It seems to me He always goes back to our hearts. He is always working from the inside out.

How do we deal with our heart issues? I believe the Scripture is clear about this. Conflict is going to happen in this life, but there's a proper way to effectively deal with it. I believe that sometimes the issue at hand just needs to be between our Savior and us. Even then we must be honest about what has happened and how it made us feel. This should always be the first step, and often I find it can and should be the only step.

What do we do if we have to take an issue to the next level? I've had a mentor for more than forty years; she helps me with my heart issues. Talking it through to get my heart right has helped me, even when I need to go to the next step, which is specified in Matthew 18:15-17:

> If your brother wrongs you, go and show him his fault, between you and him privately. If he listens to you, you have won back your brother. But if he does not listen, take along with you one or two others, so that every word may be confirmed and upheld by the testimony of two or three witnesses. If he pays no attention to them [refusing to listen and obey], tell it to the church.

The first thing to remember is that verse 15 says, "You have won back your brother." If restoration is not your goal, you might want to get your heart right first, before you open your mouth and do more damage to your relationship. My mother used to say to me, "Shelia, it's not what you said, but how you said it."

We used Matthew 18 in our home and then taught our sons

to do so as well. If our sons had a problem with one another, we taught them to go to their brother and try to talk it out. If not, then my sons could come get me to help them. When they came to me, my first question was always the same: "Have you talked with your brother about this?" If the answer was no, I would send them back to try and talk it through. If the answer was yes, I would then bring both of the boys into the same room to talk. I allowed the person who was offended to speak first. The other child was not allowed to say a word until the offended person was through. Next, the other child was allowed to tell me his side of the story. We would then try to work it out. If we could not, we tabled it until their dad got home. Then we would all four go through the same process. I remember very few times that we had to bring their father into the conversation.

I have heard my sons use this concept in dealings with those who work for them. They call it "a come-to-Jesus meeting."

TOOL 6:

Learn to Love

LEARNING TO TRULY LOVE each other is a vital concept if we and our dreamers are going to change the world with the Good News of Christ. To do that, we and they must do so from a heart filled with the love of Jesus.

Children do not come into the world loving each other. They have to be taught. Love, as described in 1 Corinthians 13, is the only acceptable response to one another. If you do not respond in love, you are in sin.

Your children will deal with their hurt in dissimilar ways. One may deal with it by stuffing it inside. You have to teach him to say, "You hurt me," and then help him choose to forgive. Another child may deal with her hurt verbally. She has to learn to be quiet and to forgive and to speak with love and kindness. Both responses—silence when words should be spoken or using hurtful words—indicate a lack of love. We as parents must teach our children to respond to one another in love and to respect the differences we all have.

They must be taught to guard their relationships. When

someone in our family hurts someone else, that person must speak to the person who was hurt and say, "I was wrong. Will you forgive me?"

When Hank and I were first married, Hank asked an older man what made a good marriage. He said, "Two very good for-givers!" I know in our family that has worked! After all, God has forgiven us all our sin. Surely we can love and forgive one another.

What about sibling rivalry? Can brothers and sisters learn to love one another and to live in peace and harmony?

First Corinthians 13:3-8 tells us what real love looks like:

> Even if I dole out all that I have [to the poor in providing] food, and if I surrender my body to be burned or in order that I may glory, but have not love (God's love in me), I gain nothing. Love endures long and is patient and kind; love never is envious nor boils over with jealousy, is not boastful or vainglorious, does not display itself haughtily. It is not conceited (arrogant and inflated with pride); it is not rude (unmannerly) and does not act unbecomingly. Love (God's love in us) does not insist on its own rights or its own way, for it is not self-seeking; it is not touchy or fretful or resentful; it takes no account of the evil done to it [it pays no attention to a suffered wrong]. It does not rejoice at injustice and unrighteousness, but rejoices when right and truth prevail. Love bears up under anything and everything that comes, is ever ready to believe the best of every person, its hopes are fadeless under all circumstances, and it endures everything [without weakening]. Love never fails [never fades out or

becomes obsolete or comes to an end]. As for prophecy (the gift of interpreting the divine will and purpose), it will be fulfilled and pass away; as for tongues, they will be destroyed and cease; as for knowledge, it will pass away [it will lose its value and be superseded by truth].

Here is a great exercise for you and your family to do together. First, put Jesus' name in the place of the word *love*. That's the easy part. Jesus is all of this. God is love. Now for the hard part. If you are a Christ follower and Christ lives in you, you have all that He is. Now put your name in the place of the word *love* and read these verses. It's really convicting.

Remember, Jesus is our standard; God is love. Christ lives in us, and by His power we can learn to love one another like this.

Love found in 1 Corinthians 13 was the only acceptable response to one another in our home. If you did not respond with love, you were in sin. Children have to be taught how to love one another. I would often go back to this passage of Scripture to remind our sons that they were not being loving.

Memorize this passage as a family. I remember one of the women I discipled had five small children, and every night at the dinner table they would recite the love chapter. She called me one morning and said she wanted me to hear her two-year-old. This toddler could not say all the words, but she had the sounds down!

As your dreamers venture out on their daring journeys and into the little-known waters of life, they will need to know how to give love to all those God brings into their lives.

TOOL 7:

Learn to Pray

TO BE EFFECTIVE IN THIS LIFE, we have to learn to pray. If our children are ever to find their God-given gifts and follow their dreams, they must be able to communicate with their Lord. The disciples asked Jesus to teach them to pray. Lord, teach us to pray!

> Then He was praying in a certain place; and when He stopped, one of His disciples said to Him, Lord, teach us to pray, [just] as John taught his disciples. And He said to them, When you pray, say: Our Father Who is in heaven, hallowed be Your name, Your kingdom come. Your will be done [held holy and revered] on earth as it is in heaven. Give us daily our bread [food for the morrow]. And forgive us our sins, for we ourselves also forgive everyone who is indebted to us [who has

offended us or done us wrong]. And bring us not into temptation but rescue us from evil.

LUKE 11:1-4

This prayer is known as the Lord's Prayer, but it might qualify as a teaching prayer. Another one of Jesus' prayers is found in John 17, just before Judas betrays Him. In the prayer, He prays for you as well as me. He gives us a model, an example—or, in modern terms, a template for prayer.

I began writing this segment on prayer while on vacation in Hawaii. We attended a Bible church there, and guess what? Greg Laurie, the pastor of Harvest Christian Fellowship, was teaching a passage on prayer. He said that the pronouns in the Lord's Prayer are plural. For example: *Our* Father, give *us*, forgive *us*, as *we*, lead *us*, and deliver *us*. This reminded me of the fact that Jesus prayed for us, and now He wants us to learn to pray together for one another as a family. He loves us individually and also as a body (His bride). Jesus prayed, "Neither pray I for these alone, but for them also which shall believe on me through their word; that they all may be one; as thou, Father, art in me, and I in thee, that they also may be one in us: that the world may believe that thou hast sent me" (John 17:20-21, KJV).

Matthew 6:1-15 is a familiar passage of Scripture to most of us. Jesus starts with what not to do. We are not to pray to be seen by others, as the hypocrites do. This does not mean that we never pray aloud, but this direction does address our hearts again. We are not to pray so that everyone thinks we are spiritual.

Jesus also said in the Sermon on the Mount not to use vain

repetitions in our prayers: "And when you pray, do not heap up empty phrases as the Gentiles do, for they think that they will be heard for their many words" (Matthew 6:7, ESV). The hypocrites loved to pray for the approval of man, and the Gentiles used empty repetitions to try to be heard by God. They are both wrong. As we pray, we need to rest in the comforting fact that He knows what we need before we ask Him.

Balance is the key to our walk with the Lord. We pray because He says, "The effectual fervent prayer of a righteous man availeth much. Elias was a man subject to like passions as we are, and he prayed earnestly that it might not rain: and it rained not on the earth by the space of three years and six months. And he prayed again, and the heaven gave rain, and the earth brought forth her fruit" (James 5:16-18, KJV).

Wow! This says that our earnest, heartfelt, continuing prayers make tremendous power available. When we pray from our hearts, somehow the power of God is released, and it is dynamic. We are once again referring to our hearts. You might wonder why. The heart is always the issue because God always looks at our hearts. He looks right through us into our innermost being and sees the truth. Just to remind myself every day, I used to have a framed verse next to my bathroom mirror that read, "Thou God seest me!" If we are walking with Him, this should comfort us because when no one else understands us, He does. He sees the truth and He cares about what He sees. He says, "Bring everything to Me." A true meaning of prayer is bringing everything to the throne of God because He cares.

How we love one another in our families, our churches, and beyond definitely reflects on Him. This is such a reminder that there is a lost and hurting world watching us to see if He is worth following. They want to see if, indeed, God hears us and loves us. Does He answer our prayers?

Let's consider some key phrases of the Lord's Prayer so we can understand how He wants us to pray.

Our Father

"Abba, Father" is a term expressing warm affection. It has no perfect equivalent in our language, but we might say "Daddy."

> And he said, Abba, Father, all things are possible unto thee; take away this cup from me: nevertheless not what I will, but what thou wilt.
>
> MARK 14:36, KJV

> For ye have not received the spirit of bondage again to fear; but ye have received the Spirit of adoption, whereby we cry, Abba, Father.
>
> ROMANS 8:15, KJV

> And because ye are sons, God hath sent forth the Spirit of his Son into your hearts, crying, Abba, Father.
>
> GALATIANS 4:6, KJV

Some of you might have a hard time relating to God as a father because of the relationship you have had with your earthly father. Maybe your father was angry, harsh, uninvolved, or absent, or maybe you could never please him. God is not any of those ways. He is a *good* Father. He is a Father who truly loves and cares about you, who wants you to run to Him in prayer. He is actually a Father who runs to you even when you are far off, just as the father does in the Prodigal Son story in Luke 15:20.

Hallowed Be Thy Name
Hallowed means "kept holy." God's name is already holy, but we must keep it holy by the way we live our lives and the way we speak of Him and about Him.

Thy Will Be Done
Thy will be done. How? "On earth as it is in heaven" (Luke 11:2). Exactly what would doing God's will look like in our lives?

I was given a great example of this about twenty years ago when Hank and I were asked by his aging Medal of Honor–recipient father to accept an acknowledgment on his behalf in Guam. The Air Force base was naming a building after him, and he was too sick to travel.

When Hank and I arrived at the base, we were introduced to a young officer who had been assigned to take care of our every need while we were there. Whenever we called him, he never said, "I'll try to get to that sometime today," or "Sorry, I don't have time for that." No, his answer was always the same thing: "Yes, sir, I'll get on that right now."

Not only did he say he would do it; he did whatever it was in record time. He even listened to our conversation as we passed a doughnut shop and Hank said, "Boy, I would love to have some doughnuts." Next thing we knew, he showed up with a dozen fresh doughnuts. He always ended with the same remark: "Sir, is there anything else, sir?"

I believe that is how the Father's will is done in heaven, and He wants us to do the same here on earth. I really do not think there is any slow obedience in heaven. He wants us to desire His will more than we want our own way. You must ask yourself, is He your genie or your God? In other words, is He there to give us everything we want, or is He God in our lives and are we therefore to obey just like that young officer in Guam?

I delight to do Your will, O my God; yes, Your law is within my heart.

PSALM 40:8

Saying, Father, if You are willing, remove this cup from Me; yet not My will, but [always] Yours be done.

LUKE 22:42

Do not be conformed to this world (this age), [fashioned after and adapted to its external, superficial customs], but be transformed (changed) by the [entire] renewal of your mind [by its new ideals and its new attitude], so that you may prove [for yourselves] what is the good and acceptable and perfect will of God, even the thing which is good and acceptable and perfect [in His sight for you].

ROMANS 12:2

Therefore do not be vague and thoughtless and foolish, but understanding and firmly grasping what the will of the Lord is.

EPHESIANS 5:17

Give Us This Day

Trust God one day at a time. He wants us to aim for Him as well as His Kingdom, His righteousness, His way of doing things, and being right with Him. We have only this moment. That is all we can see, but we can trust in Him because He can see forever.

Not trusting means having little or no faith in Him and leads to fear, which causes us to act like lost people. We can trust Him because He knows what we need and when we need it. Life is not about things. Real life is found in seeking His Kingdom and His righteousness. He knows that we need things to be able to live in this world, and He will give them to us. He is a good Father, and He loves us all. Simply trust Him.

> Wherefore, if God so clothe the grass of the field,
> which to day is, and to morrow is cast into the oven,
> shall he not much more clothe you, O ye of little faith?
> Therefore take no thought, saying, What shall we eat?
> or, What shall we drink? or, Wherewithal shall we be
> clothed? (For after all these things do the Gentiles
> seek:) for your heavenly Father knoweth that ye have
> need of all these things. But seek ye first the kingdom
> of God, and his righteousness; and all these things shall
> be added unto you.
>
> MATTHEW 6:30-33, KJV

Forgive Us

We must learn to live in His forgiveness. Remember, we have been made clean by His death, and we may be kept clean through His life as we walk in this world.

We Forgive

Our forgiving others is to protect our redeemed hearts so that hurt cannot take root in them. We all know how hard a weed is to get rid of when it has deep roots; so is bitterness hard to get out of our hearts if we let it grow roots.

Forgiveness means we are releasing the person who hurt us from the effects of that hurt in our lives. It does not always mean that there will be restoration or that you will trust them again. Sometimes that happens, but sometimes it means that you are going to just let it go.

> If possible, as far as it depends on you, live at peace with everyone.
>
> ROMANS 12:18

> Exercise foresight and be on the watch to look
> [after one another], to see that no one falls back
> from and fails to secure God's grace (His un-
> merited favor and spiritual blessing), in order
> that no root of resentment (rancor, bitterness, or
> hatred) shoots forth and causes trouble and bitter
> torment, and the many become contaminated
> and defiled by it.
>
> HEBREWS 12:15

Lead Us

> He refreshes and restores my life (my self); He leads
> me in the paths of righteousness [uprightness and

right standing with Him—not for my earning it,
but] for His name's sake.

PSALM 23:3

Deliver Us

Who gave (yielded) Himself up [to atone] for our
sins [and to save and sanctify us], in order to rescue
and deliver us from this present wicked age and world
order, in accordance with the will and purpose and
plan of our God and Father.

GALATIANS 1:4

Power and Glory

To Him [be ascribed all] the glory through all the ages
of the ages and the eternities of the eternities! Amen
(so be it).

GALATIANS 1:5

He leads us and delivers us by His power into His glory.
And then we will rejoice! In fact, He tells us to rejoice always.

Have you asked Him to teach you to pray? Do you pray as
a family? We did. We had a prayer altar in our home. It was the
large coffee table in our den. At night, after Hank read the Bible,
he would start with Jon, asking if he had any needs, and then
asking each of us the same question. Then we would write down
our responses to pray about them. I have often wished we had
kept a prayer journal and written down each answered prayer.

One important thing we taught our sons about prayer is that God answers *all* of our prayers. We used a common traffic light to teach them this concept. When the light is red, it means no. Yes, *no* is an answer. We often think that the only answer to our prayers is yes. That is just not true. Think about Paul. He begged the Lord three times to remove the thorn in the flesh, and God's answer was "No, My grace will cover that."

If the light is green, that means the answer is yes. This is the answer we all like to hear. But Psalm 106:15 says, "He gave them their request, but sent leanness into their souls." So my prayer has always been, "Lord, no matter what I do or say, if yes will bring leanness to my soul, do not give it to me."

But there is another light. The yellow one, in the middle. What does that mean? It means caution . . . slow down and wait. This is our least favorite light, but it's still important.

Adventures in Prayer

Prayer is one way to make daily deposits in our children's lives. If they had a need and did not have a way to meet that need, we taught them that the situation was going to be a great adventure and a new way to see God provide. As parents, we have always tried to teach our children that God cares about them and their personal needs.

Learning to pray and seeing God provide is an important exercise of faith for the future of your creative child. The Lord can use prayer to build their faith and trust in Him. In the Old Testament, God's people were instructed to stack stones up as a reminder of God's faithfulness, and when they passed by them, they were to tell their children the story behind the stones.

When your children are adults and are faced with a need,

they can draw from the trust He built in them as children through answered prayer.

At night right before bedtime, we would kneel as a family and pray, and we would each have a turn. I would like to share just a few of the answers to prayer we've seen as a family.

⟶

Hank has always said that if a person wants something done, ask a child to pray for it. I remember a time this happened to us.

It was in October 1985. We were looking forward to a lot of activity. Hank was on staff at a local church and was going to El Salvador on a mission trip in December, and Andy was going to be a toy soldier in the Christmas play. We were renting a wonderful house only a little way from the church, at an unbelievably low price. Everything was great.

One Saturday morning we got the news that the lady we were renting our house from needed it back for her parents. This meant we had ninety days to find a new place to live.

Since we had always been in the ministry, we had put to death the idea of owning our own home. As things progressed, though, we found that thanks to those who loved us, home ownership might become a reality.

As was our custom, we called our boys, Andy, age nine, and Jon, age five, into the den to talk and pray about buying a home of our own. I told everyone to think about what kind of house they wanted. Hank grabbed a pencil and paper, and we made a list. I asked for a formal living room, a dining room, and a den. Hank asked for a flat yard. Then it was the boys' turn! They asked for a tree house and, of all things, a swimming pool.

Hank and I, being the giants in the faith that we are, looked at each other with horror. We knew just how much we could pay for a house. Being realistic adults, we knew finding a nice house for that price was going to be a task, even without a pool and a tree house. We had taught our children that God could do anything, so we were on the spot. We prayed, "If it be Your will," just to give God an out. This is sad but true. Our boys did not pray that kind of prayer that night. They prayed asking in faith for their pool and tree house, telling God in detail what they wanted each to look like.

Weeks went by. We looked and looked, only to be disappointed. We finally found a house where we could live. It was not what we had prayed for. It had no flat yard, no living room, and of course no pool or tree house. And it was more than we had said that we could pay.

Hank and I decided that it was our only option. He told me to call the real estate agent the next day and have her put a contract on it. He then picked up a newspaper and out of habit began to look at the want ads. He stopped reading and called out to me. He said, "Shelia, listen to this," and then read the listing in the newspaper. "It sounds like someone has been reading our prayer requests," he concluded. There it was: a formal living room, formal dining room, large den, three bedrooms, two baths, flat yard, in-ground pool, and, oh yes, a nice tree house, just like our boys had described to God in their prayers! But best of all, the price was what we had agreed on.

As we looked at each other in disbelief, Hank spoke first. "I wonder if this is our house. Go look at it first thing in the morning, and if you like it, we will buy it."

I called my real estate agent, and she told me not to get my hopes up because the deal seemed too good to be true. I drove to the place early the next morning, and as I stood in the dining room, I knew it was our house.

What a mighty God we have! How wonderful are the prayers of His little ones. He searches to and fro to find one man, woman, or child to whom He might show Himself strong. For almost a year after that, every time we drove into the driveway of our new home, Andy and Jon would say, "Mom, look at our house. Can you believe what God did?"

⁓

Hank says one of the hardest things a human can trust God for is money, and we're no exception. One day our ministry needed $2,000. We had a deadline to meet, we had waited out the month, and the coffers were dry. Hank called the family into the den and prayed, "Lord, we need $2,000 today!" We didn't tell anyone about the need.

Hank went to the post office with fear and trembling, and there was one lonely envelope in our box. This was it! It was all or nothing. He opened it holding his breath. It was a check for exactly $2,000!

⁓

"Dad, I've lost my wallet," five-year-old Jon said. "I don't know where it is, and it has twenty dollars inside!" Hank didn't know where it was either. He had seen it on the dining room table but didn't know what had happened to it. The only thing I knew to do was call our family to prayer.

Jon was obviously discouraged, but Hank said, "God knows where it is! He can help you find it." Hank had the entire family gather in the den. We joined hands and prayed, "Lord, Jon has lost his wallet with twenty dollars inside. It's somewhere in this house, but we don't know where. Could You find it for us? And thank You for Your help! Amen." Then Jon prayed, "God, will You please find my wallet for me?"

After that prayer, we just let it go. We didn't fret or worry. We went about our everyday business.

Two weeks later, Jon called Hank at the office. With sheer delight he said, "Dad, guess what? The Lord found my wallet!"

Hank said, "Praise the Lord! Where did you find it?"

It had fallen behind Jon's desk.

"If we had not prayed," Jon said, "I would never have thought to look there. God did it!"

It's often said that God works in mysterious ways. Sometimes He even uses a dog to answer prayer!

In 1986, Jon was going to celebrate his fourth birthday. I had scheduled a festive birthday party with all the trimmings at McDonald's. The birthday cake had been ordered, and the crowd was scheduled to gather at 2:00 p.m.

Two hours before the party, I told Hank that we needed twenty dollars to pay for the party and the cake. The only problem was that we were plumb broke at the time. Funds were stretched to the max. We didn't even have two cents to our name on that day.

"Twenty dollars!" came Hank's stunned reply. "I thought the

party had already been paid for. We don't have twenty dollars! Payday is next week. I don't know what we're going to do!"

Timidly I said, "Maybe we should pray?"

In Hank's heart he thought, *What good would that do at a time like this?* But with great apprehension, we gathered the family in the living room and all joined hands and prayed, "Lord, we need twenty dollars now! Jon's birthday party is in two hours, and we need to pay for it. Please help us now."

He thought this would be a surefire failure of a prayer. We had not given God any slack before our observant children.

As soon as Hank said amen, my mother's dog, Bo, jumped to his feet and raced bathroom-call style to the door. Hank was ticked off! Here was a prayer crisis, and of all things, Bo had to go for a walk! With sheer irritation, he attached the leash to Bo and opened the door. "I'll take the dog," he said, "and maybe I can think of something!"

We were keeping Bo while my parents were on vacation. A snow-white poodle with a feisty, perky personality, he was hard to keep in the yard. He loved to roam and explore. Left alone outside, he often became an instant runaway. And all that week, he had developed a path. He would walk down the block, turn right, and go farther down the street.

However, in this instance he did an odd thing—and he was in a frenzy! He was a dog on a mission, his stubby little tail wagging like a windup top spinning at superspeed. Instead of turning right at the end of the block, he turned left and went up the street. Hank, totally perturbed, asked Bo, "Where are you going?" Bo didn't even look back. Halfway down the block, the dog turned into a dirt alley running into an undeveloped plot of land covered with bushes.

Hank huffed, "This is ridiculous! A snakebite is all I need to top off this day!"

Bo was undaunted. Halfway into the vacant lot, as Hank was being dragged along toward a tree, to his astonishment, he saw an absolutely unbelievable sight! At the base of the tree was some money. He jerked on Bo's leash and screamed, "No, Bo!" He had to get that money before Bo got to the tree. Hank reached down and picked up a genuine American greenback—a twenty-dollar bill! He was flabbergasted. Then he giggled like a child. He had twenty dollars! The still, small voice of God in his ear called in quiet rebuke, "I'm still in business! I can still provide!"

In repentance Hank replied, "Yes, sir," as he returned home with great joy. Exactly two hours later, we had Jon's party paid for in cash—we were saved through prayer and a poodle!

~∽

I remember one opportunity I had to teach Andy about prayer. He was about nine years old. I came into his room to tuck him in and pray with him. Looking at him on the top bunk, I saw his countenance had fallen.

I asked him what was wrong, and he smiled and said, "Oh, nothing, and anyway it doesn't matter." I told him it did matter, and that I wanted to know why he felt hurt.

He then began to tell me that at school (this was before we were homeschooling) some boys made fun of his off-brand tennis shoes. I asked him how that made him feel, and he said it made him so sad. He quickly said, "Oh, Mom, I really don't mind the shoes. It's really okay."

I then asked him if he wanted some Nike tennis shoes. He said, "Mom, I'm thankful to the Lord that I have tennis shoes. It's really okay."

I took his face in my hands and said, "Andrew, I know your walk with the Lord, and I know you will accept whatever He gives you, but that was not the question. I asked you, would you like to have some Nike tennis shoes?"

His answer was, "Well, I guess so!"

We were on church staff, and Andy and I both knew that Nike shoes were not in our budget. He also knew that his parents would not spend seventy-five dollars of the Lord's money on tennis shoes for a nine-year-old who would outgrow them in two months. Our budget only allowed for twenty dollars for this project.

I don't know if he thought I was going to say, "We'll go first thing in the morning, and I'll use my grocery money—" this was a temptation for me—"so you can buy any shoes your heart desires." Thank goodness I didn't say that, because if I had, my son would not have been able to see how much God loves him.

What I did say that day was, "Andy, twenty dollars is all the Lord has provided for tennis shoes. I tell you what I'll do: I will pray with you that God will provide Nikes for twenty dollars." So we bowed our heads, and Andy told the Lord that he would be content with whatever He gave him, but that he really would like to have some Nikes.

The next morning, as Hank was reading the newspaper, Andy and I glanced at the back of it and then did a double take. Can you guess what we saw? There was an ad for a sale on Nike shoes for $19.95. We purchased them that afternoon. Yes,

God does care about tennis shoes—especially if through giving them He can show Himself faithful to a little boy.

⟿

These are just a few examples of how God has been so faithful to show Himself strong to our children. Sometimes He has given them what they wanted, and sometimes He has shown them that they really didn't need what they thought they did.

Seeing my children bend the knee to God's will has been one of the most wonderful joys of my life. I guess the one thing that we've learned as a family is that He's a wonderful Savior and has a wonderful plan for our lives.

Now, as grown men, they are teaching their own children of God's faithfulness. As the heads of Kingdom Story Company, they are having to trust God with a lot more than lost wallets and Nike tennis shoes.

Teach your children to pray. Who knows? One day they might need to see God provide $2 million in two weeks to get their movie in the theaters. They might even be backed up to the Red Sea with an Egyptian army in hot pursuit. They will need to know how to pray because they will need God to part the waters for them.

TOOL 8:

Be Armed for Battle

HOW CAN WE TEACH OUR DREAMERS to withstand incredible
pressures, not be defeated, and emerge victorious? They need
a divine and unbeatable defense: the armor of God. What is
the armor of God? There are many good books written on this
subject, but I want to just introduce you to the fact that we are
given the armor of God.

> The night is far gone and the day is almost here. Let us
> then drop (fling away) the works and deeds of darkness
> and put on the [full] armor of light. Let us live and
> conduct ourselves honorably and becomingly as in
> the [open light of] day, not in reveling (carousing)
> and drunkenness, not in immorality and debauchery
> (sensuality and licentiousness), not in quarreling and
> jealousy. But clothe yourself with the Lord Jesus Christ
> (the Messiah), and make no provision for [indulging]
> the flesh [put a stop to thinking about the evil cravings
> of your physical nature] to [gratify its] desires (lusts).
> ROMANS 13:12-14

In conclusion, be strong in the Lord [be empowered through your union with Him]; draw your strength from Him [that strength which His boundless might provides]. Put on God's whole armor [the armor of a heavy-armed soldier which God supplies], that you may be able successfully to stand up against [all] the strategies and the deceits of the devil. For we are not wrestling with flesh and blood [contending only with physical opponents], but against the despotisms, against the powers, against [the master spirits who are] the world rulers of this present darkness, against the spirit forces of wickedness in the heavenly (supernatural) sphere. Therefore put on God's complete armor, that you may be able to resist and stand your ground on the evil day [of danger], and, having done all [the crisis demands], to stand [firmly in your place]. Stand therefore [hold your ground], having tightened the belt of truth around your loins and having put on the breastplate of integrity and of moral rectitude and right standing with God, and having shod your feet in preparation [to face the enemy with the firm-footed stability, the promptness, and the readiness produced by the good news] of the Gospel of peace. Lift up over all the [covering] shield of saving faith, upon which you can quench all the flaming missiles of the wicked [one]. And take the helmet of salvation and the sword that the Spirit wields, which is the Word of God. Pray at all times (on every occasion, in every season) in the Spirit, with all [manner of] prayer and entreaty. To that end keep alert and watch with strong purpose and perseverance, interceding in behalf of all the saints (God's consecrated people).

EPHESIANS 6:10-18

The stakes are higher than they have ever been in our lives, so first we are to be clothed with the Lord Jesus Christ and be strong in Him. Then we are to put on God's complete armor, which our union with Him provides.

Our armor consists of the helmet of salvation, the shield of faith, the breastplate of righteousness, the belt of truth, and the sword of the Spirit.

After we have prepared for battle and have put on our armor, what are we to do next? Stand. Wearing our armor, we are to resist and to stand firmly in our place.

King Jehoshaphat is one of the best examples of how we are to do battle. He had set his heart to seek God, and then he organized everything in his kingdom around the Lord, reminding all of his people to fear the Lord. He had prepared them to serve the Lord, and . . .

Now it happened after this that the Moabites and the Ammonites, together with some of the Meunites, came to make war against Jehoshaphat. Then it was reported to Jehoshaphat, "A great multitude has come against you from beyond the [Dead] Sea, out of Aram (Syria); and behold, they are in Hazazon-tamar (that is, Engedi)."

2 CHRONICLES 20:1-2, AMP

He had done things right, and now he was being surrounded by his enemies. What was his response to this message? He was afraid.

You know what? There are things in life to be afraid of. One of the verses I taught our sons about fear was "When I am afraid, I put my trust in you" (Psalm 56:3, ESV). It does not say *if* I am afraid; it says *when* I am afraid. There are going to be times in your life when you are afraid, but the most important thing is what you do when you are afraid. Do you put your trust in God?

I am bent to fear. When I was twenty-seven years old, my healthy fifty-four-year-old father died. Hank and I were living in Dallas, and we went home to be with my mom. This happened the first week in December, and we were going to stay with her until January, but Hank had to fly back to Dallas to take his finals. I was left alone to be with Mom.

The night after Hank left, my mom began to have chest pains, so I called our neighbor, who was a doctor. He thought it would be a good idea to take her to the emergency room.

After running some tests, even though they did not think it was her heart, they decided they should keep her there overnight. At that point, fear of losing her began to grip my heart. After all, I had just lost one parent.

The neighbors invited me to stay with them overnight. They had a large home, and I was in the guest room down a hallway that seemed a mile long.

That night was one of the hardest I've ever experienced in my life. I have never felt so alone and afraid. All I could do was cry out to the Lord and read the Psalms. I would feel comforted and fall asleep only to be awakened by my fear. I repeated that process all night long. I have never been so happy to see the sunrise.

I made it through the night, and later that morning found

out Mom was doing just fine. That night I learned that God could get me though the darkest hours.

The devil roars accusations in our ear. He knows our vulnerabilities. He tells us we are useless, weak, a failure, a disappointment to God, and not even worthy of being a mom. First Peter 5:8 says, "Be well balanced (temperate, sober of mind), be vigilant and cautious at all times; for that enemy of yours, the devil, roams around like a lion roaring [in fierce hunger], seeking someone to seize upon and devour." Satan wants us to be discouraged, distraught, disappointed, disconnected, downcast, depressed, dejected, distrusting, and defeated—but most of all he wants to destroy us.

What is his best weapon? It is fear, fear that causes us to distrust God. Even as he knows our vulnerabilities, do you know where you are most vulnerable? What are you afraid of? Whatever it is, bring it to the great I Am.

Casting the whole of your care [all your anxieties, all your worries, all your concerns, once and for all] on Him, for He cares for you affectionately and cares about you watchfully.

1 PETER 5:7

Then Jehoshaphat feared, and set himself [determinedly, as his vital need] to seek the Lord; he proclaimed a fast in all Judah. And Judah gathered together to ask help from the Lord; even out of all the cities of Judah they came to seek the Lord [yearning for Him with all their desire].

2 CHRONICLES 20:3-4

For as he thinks in his heart, so is he.

PROVERBS 23:7

The first thing Jehoshaphat did was to take care of his own heart. He sought the Lord because of his great need. This does not say that he said to himself, *There is nothing to be afraid of,* or *Man up and stop being afraid.* No, he was afraid, so he did the right thing. He cast his fear on the Lord. Psalm 56:3-4 says, "When I am afraid, I put my trust in you. In God, whose word I praise, in God I trust; I shall not be afraid. What can flesh do to me?" (ESV).

Jehoshaphat's faith was not in his strength or his courage. His faith did not focus on the problem or the circumstances. No, he focused on God and believed God in spite of his circumstances. Then he obeyed God one step at a time. Then he addressed the nation. He asked them to fast and to ask God for help. Because of his leadership in days past, they came and sought the Lord with their whole hearts. Second Chronicles 20:5 says, "And Jehoshaphat stood in the assembly of Judah and Jerusalem in the house of the Lord before the new court." Then Jehoshaphat stood, and he prayed. In his prayer he reminded God, himself, and all those gathered of just who God is.

> And said, O Lord, God of our fathers, are You not God in heaven? And do You not rule over all the kingdoms of the nations? In Your hand are power and might, so that none is able to withstand You.
>
> Did not You, O our God, drive out the inhabitants of this land before Your people Israel and give it forever to the descendants of Abraham Your friend? They

dwelt in it and have built You a sanctuary in it for
Your Name, saying, If evil comes upon us, the sword
of judgment, or pestilence, or famine, we will stand
before this house and before You—for Your Name [and
the symbol of Your presence] is in this house—and cry
to You in our affliction, and You will hear and save.

2 CHRONICLES 20:6-9

He talked about the greatness of God. He did not spend
hours researching the enemy and telling the people how
powerful they were. He meditated on what he knew about who
God is. These are the things that would give him faith and
hope. As believers, we must know what God has promised and
learn to rest in His promises and provisions.

I believe it is dangerous to become fascinated with our
enemy and attempt to become an expert in knowing all about
him, but it is just as dangerous to live as if we have no enemy.
The balance is to acknowledge that we have an enemy and then
to proclaim that we have victory though the great I AM.

Jehoshaphat also reminded God that His sovereign hand
had been at work in this as well.

And now behold, the men of Ammon, Moab, and
Mount Seir, whom You would not let Israel invade
when they came from the land of Egypt, and whom
they turned from and did not destroy—
    Behold, they reward us by coming to drive us out of
Your possession which You have given us to inherit. O
our God, will You not exercise judgment upon them?

2 CHRONICLES 20:10-12

What a king he was! He cast himself entirely upon the Lord in a helpless situation. Basically, he said, "God, this is too big for us, and if you don't show up, we are dead." Have you ever been in a God-if-you-don't-show-up-we-are-dead place?

> For we have no might to stand against this great
> company that is coming against us. We do not know
> what to do, but our eyes are upon You.
>
> 2 CHRONICLES 20:12

Now it was God's turn to talk. So what was His answer?

> And all Judah stood before the Lord, with their children
> and their wives. Then the Spirit of the Lord came upon
> Jahaziel son of Zechariah, the son of Benaiah, the son of
> Jeiel, the son of Mattaniah, a Levite of the sons of Asaph,
> in the midst of the assembly. He said, Hearken, all Judah,
> you inhabitants of Jerusalem, and you King Jehoshaphat.
> The Lord says this to you: Be not afraid or dismayed at
> this great multitude; for the battle is not yours, but God's.
>
> 2 CHRONICLES 20:13-15

God first addresses Jehoshaphat's fear by reminding him that the battle is not his but the Lord's. The Bible says, "fear not," or "be not afraid" more than one hundred times. The Lord does not want us to be afraid. In fact, He tells us that perfect love casts out fear. Then He gives them instructions: "Tomorrow go down to them. Behold, they will come up by the Ascent of Ziz, and you will find them at the end of the ravine before the Wilderness of Jeruel" (2 Chronicles 20:16).

Oh dear. Get up and go face them! Go face your fears. This would not be my first choice. (You see, I am a coward! In fact, two of my favorite gifts from my dear husband are a doll and a statue of the Cowardly Lion from *The Wizard of Oz*.) This might not have been their first choice either. But God told them this: "You shall not need to fight in this battle; take your positions, stand still, and see the deliverance of the Lord [Who is] with you, O Judah and Jerusalem. Fear not nor be dismayed. Tomorrow go out against them, for the Lord is with you" (2 Chronicles 20:17).

Then He gives them detailed instructions while reminding them that they will not need to fight in this battle. If they're not going to have to fight, what are they going to have to do? They are to take their positions as if they are going to fight. Then what? They are to just stand there.

Couldn't God just take care of this without them? If they were not going to fight, God did not even need for them to be there, right? Then why did He instruct them to go and just stand there? Because God wanted them to see the deliverance that only He could give. Then He said, "I want you to trust that I Am with you."

> And Jehoshaphat bowed his head with his face to the
> ground, and all Judah and the inhabitants of Jerusalem
> fell down before the Lord, worshiping Him. And some
> Levites of the Kohathites and Korahites stood up to
> praise the Lord, the God of Israel, with a very loud voice.
> 2 CHRONICLES 20:18-19

They believed, and their response was worship and praise.

And they rose early in the morning and went out
into the Wilderness of Tekoa; and as they went out,
Jehoshaphat stood and said, Hear me, O Judah, and
you inhabitants of Jerusalem! Believe in the Lord your
God and you shall be established; believe and remain
steadfast to His prophets and you shall prosper.

2 CHRONICLES 20:20

God is saying, "Believe in Me, rest in Me, and believe My
Word, and you will be established." They demonstrated their
trust by doing what He said for them to do: They got up and
started walking.

When he had consulted with the people, he appointed
singers to sing to the Lord and praise Him in their holy
[priestly] garments as they went out before the army,
saying, Give thanks to the Lord, for His mercy and
loving-kindness endure forever!

2 CHRONICLES 20:21

This is not the usual way to organize an army. Think about
it! If you were a king taking your people into battle and they
asked, "So what are we going to do this morning?" how would
you answer? This king's answer was to sing praise to the Lord.
That is just what Jehoshaphat told them to do, and as they
obeyed, God started working.

And when they began to sing and to praise, the Lord set
ambushments against the men of Ammon, Moab, and
Mount Seir who had come against Judah, and they were

[self-] slaughtered; for [suspecting betrayal] the men of
Ammon and Moab rose against those of Mount Seir,
utterly destroying them. And when they had made an end
of the men of Seir, they all helped to destroy one another.

2 CHRONICLES 20:22-23

When did God act on their behalf? He moved when they
moved. They got up and did what He said to do. Then when
they got there, they saw what God had done.

And when Judah came to the watchtower of the
wilderness, they looked at the multitude, and behold,
they were dead bodies fallen to the earth, and none had
escaped! When Jehoshaphat and his people came to take
the spoil, they found among them much cattle, goods,
garments, and precious things which they took for
themselves, more than they could carry away, so much
they were three days in gathering the spoil. On the fourth
day they assembled in the Valley of Beracah. There they
blessed the Lord. So the name of the place is still called
the Valley of Beracah [blessing]. Then they returned,
every man of Judah and Jerusalem, Jehoshaphat leading
them, to Jerusalem with joy, for the Lord had made them
to rejoice over their enemies. They came to Jerusalem
with harps, lyres, and trumpets to the house of the Lord.
And the fear of God came upon all the kingdoms of
those countries when they heard that the Lord had fought
against the enemies of Israel. So the realm of Jehoshaphat
was quiet, for his God gave him rest round about.

2 CHRONICLES 20:24-30

What looked like defeat became a place of blessing as they rejoiced over their enemies. The best part was that all the other kingdoms saw that the Lord had fought for them and Jehoshaphat's realm was one of quiet and rest.

The truth about warfare is that we don't stand alone on the battlefield. Christ has won the victory, and His victory is our victory; therefore, we don't fight *for* victory, we fight *from* victory. We get this call to arms, and we are called to stand and watch because the battle is His.

Philip Nation, vice president, publisher for Thomas Nelson Bibles, calls God our Warrior King, writing that "spiritual battle rages around us. So fierce that God entered the battlefield to protect us: Warrior King! . . . We serve a Warrior King who does not fear darkness or death."[1]

We are to stand in the truth of who God is and how He loves us. We are to stand in His righteousness that He has given us. We are to take a stand in God's Word.

We must be armed with the Word of God. We have to read, study, memorize, and then live by it through the power of the Holy Spirit. Then we must take our stand in God's Word. Remember, it contains the full counsel of God. It is how He reveals Himself to us. It is the truth.

TOOL 9:

Life Is a Great Adventure

HANK GETS THE CREDIT for our family motto, "Life is a great adventure." He always says, "The dictionary defines the word *adventure* as 'an exciting or dangerous experience.'" He really believes that life is a great adventure, and he continues to live his life that way. He dreams big dreams and truly believes that God can do the impossible.

Our children heard this phrase constantly in our home. Whether it was something wonderful to be enjoyed or something hard to face, Hank would smile and say, "This is a great adventure." Our children quickly learned that what that meant was, "I wonder what God is going to do, or better yet, what He has already done." Scripture teaches us that He has prepared good works for us to walk in. Ephesians 2:10 says, "For we are his workmanship, created in Christ Jesus for good works, which God prepared beforehand, that we should walk in them" (ESV).

What I hear in this motto is that God is good and in absolute control. I hear His love and His provision. It is a reminder to me that I can trust Him no matter what the circumstances are and that with Him life is worth living. We can find adventure in His grace, love, and provision. He wants us to enjoy the life He provides for us through the gift of His Son. He has promised us an abundant life, a life with Jesus that is full of wonders.

When I hear "Life is a great adventure," I also understand that an adventure is not always fun and games but can be an upcoming challenge that requires hard work and determination. Our boys also understood this. When they were small, I remember once when Hank, in typical form, was beginning to say, "This is going to be a great adventure," and simultaneously both boys said, "No! Please don't say this is a great adventure." We all laughed and braced ourselves for the challenge to come.

Another adventure we experienced took place in the middle of the night. The phone rang, giving us the news that Hank's dad was on the way to the hospital. We learned later in the day that he had suffered a stroke. When I returned home, Hank shared, "Dad is about to embark on a great adventure, and we are too."

We Erwins define adventure as a place we have never walked before, yet a place Jesus knows all about. It is a place of hard work and determination, a place that works for the good of all, a place filled with God's glory, and a place that builds character in each of us. It is a new place that might even reveal a lack of character in need of correction and the Master's touch.

One night on Hank's live cable TV show, just ten minutes before showtime, he discovered that the headphones had been left at another studio. I asked him what he was going to do about the sound room not being able to communicate with the floor manager. Hank, knowing full well there was nothing else he could do, smiled at me and said, "Isn't this going to be a great adventure?" I knew then that somehow everything would be okay, and that Jesus was big enough for the task!

What is the adventure that God has entrusted to you? He is big enough for the task!

TOOL 10:

Give God Your Yes

NEVER GIVE UP. Remember, He fights for you, strengthens you, and encourages you. Don't you ever give up. Repeat this out loud: "I am not going to hell." Say it out loud . . . louder, and louder. Let it be earsplitting: "I am not going to hell, and I am bound for heaven!" Remember that on your journey God has promised you an abundant life, and He allows you to be a small part of His earthly work. When you are feeling weak and overwhelmed, lift up your head, look full in His wonderful face, and never give up!

Here's a fragment of something Hank once wrote about the Woodlawn football team:

> The defining moment of the entire Woodlawn football story was not in the movie. It happened on the team bus right after the first game of the 1973 season. Our team had just experienced revival. We had committed ourselves that season to playing for a higher purpose

than just winning. We pledged to play for the glory of God and to use football to make Jesus known.

Then we promptly went out and lost our first game. We played our hearts out against Ensley and held the four-touchdown favorite scoreless until the final moment of the game when they scored a desperation touchdown and beat us 7–3.

When we went back to get on the team bus after the game, there was a noticeable chilly silence. Nobody said a word. It was an icy-cold grim mood. I sat next to the head coach, Tandy Gerelds, on the front row of the bus. He was not happy when I took my seat. He had not bought into Jesus yet. He did not want to commit his life to something he could not see. I guess you could say he was a true skeptic and cynic.

When I sat down next to him on the bus, he nudged me on the arm, and in a low-growl voice said, "You have got to say something to the team. They thought they were going to win because they were playing for Jesus. Now their hearts are broken. They could all quit. You have to say something right now!" I prayed a quick prayer for help, stood up, turned around, and faced the team. Every eye of the bus was on me. I knew that whatever I said in the next two minutes would be the biggest speech that I ever gave in my life. I told them, "Fellows, there is one thing that I didn't tell you about this commitment to play for Jesus. With every commitment, there is a test to see what your true motivation is. If you think that committing to play for Jesus is going to get you a genie, a rabbit's foot, or a lucky charm to just help you win football games, it is not going to work. God is not going to be a genie! He is going to be God when you win and when you lose. If you are going to play for Him, you will have to give Him praise when you win and give Him praise when you lose. You need to make up your mind right now. If you just want a genie, we might as well fold it up and go home, because it is not going to work. God is not going to be a genie. So make up your mind right now. It's either all in, or all out."

I waited. For about twenty seconds, nothing happened. Just cold silence. Then from the back of the bus, a lone voice spoke up, "I'm still in!" And then another voice chimed in saying, "I'm still in!" And then players all over the bus began to nod their heads in agreement and started saying, "I'm still in!" Then all of a sudden, they started to chant, "We're still in! Still in!" Then it changed to "All in! All in! All in! All in!" It got louder and louder until it rocked the bus. The whole mood changed from gloom to all-out determination to play for the glory of God, no matter what the cost.

Finally, I put my hands up to calm the noise down, and I said, "All right, now let's go home and go to work." So we went home, went to work, and we started to run the table and win. They played so far above their abilities and won games so far beyond explanation that the rest of the 1973 season became a legend in Birmingham high school football folklore. The Woodlawn football team proved that amazing things can happen to anyone who makes a decision for Jesus, catches the vision of living for a high purpose in life, and truly gets all in!

Are you all in? You must make up your mind right now. It's either all in, or all out. The real question is, are you for God or against Him? Give God your yes.

One day I was out shopping with a dear friend and prayer partner of mine who had been in my Bible study, when she suddenly said, "Shelia, I finally understand! When something comes up in your life that requires obedience, you do not have to decide whether you will obey or not. You have already made the decision to make Jesus Lord of your life—there are no exceptions—and you walk by the decision you've already made. Understanding this has changed my life." She explained that up until that realization she had been arguing with God every time some decision came up. She had been selective on what she would and would not obey, similar to choosing items in a grocery store, instead of yielding and obeying.

Have you decided that you will obey, or do you think you have the right to debate Him on every command? This does not mean that there will not be challenges as you change and are being conformed to God's image, but are you yielded to Him and walking in obedience to Him? If your dreamers give God their yes, God will lead them into His plan for their lives.

⟶๑๑

Thank you for sitting at my kitchen table and hearing my heart. I feel a little bit sad that we have come to the end of our look at how to find and grow your child's God-given talents. I can't help but wonder what you have gleaned from our time together. I pray you have come to know, trust, and love God better as you are raising up your dreamers.

I know that so often we are looking for that magic formula that will guarantee our children's success in life, free of pain, as well as for our own validation as moms. There is no such thing. We live in a broken world with broken people. In fact, before we became Christ followers, we were broken. In our journey of life there will be success and failure. As a mother, you will experience unbelievable joys. There will be those worth-it moments as you navigate through your journey, but there will also be times of heartache. Moms, you are forever connected to your child. When they rejoice, you will rejoice with them, but when they hurt, you will also hurt, sometimes to the very bottom of your soul. May I remind you that for this you have Jesus, and He's working all things together for your good and His glory, and that is also true for your child.

Remember the man who said I was wasting my education? Here's what Jon has to say about that.

Have you ever been told you weren't normal? That you didn't fit in? Well . . . that's exactly what was said to a wide-eyed, ADHD bundle of rambunctiousness named Jon. Even though I was making A's and B's, for the sake of everyone else's sanity, I was told I had to do kindergarten AGAIN because I was a "disturbance to the class."

Faced with this situation, my mom made a very brave decision and decided to homeschool my brother and me. This was no easy task. My attention span was about thirty seconds, and I had more nervous energy than the squirrel from *Ice Age*. It didn't faze my mom, though, and she began to help me learn in a different way. In my own way.

When I was fifteen, something extraordinary happened. For over a year, I had been interning for a broadcast cameraman named Mike who went to my church. On a beautiful fall Saturday, he called me and said that a cameraman on a local ESPN college football game was sick and they desperately needed a replacement. Then he said, "Jon, I've talked to the director. Get over here as fast as you can! Don't tell anyone how old you are!" I was nervous, but I will always remember that moment when I put on the headphones and unlocked the tripod to the massive, telescope-style camera. That was the moment I fell in love with what would become my career and life's calling. . . .

The next year my dad bought my brother and me a professional camera and helped us get a loan. All of a sudden, at sixteen years old, we had our own video production company! Our hobby quickly grew out of control. Then, after a decade of commercials, award-winning music videos, documentaries, and TV pilots, I was challenged to "discover a purpose to our work" by director Alex Kendrick while working for him on the movie *Courageous*. So we shifted our focus to tell our own stories, instead of just being a hired gun. This led us to our true love: feature films.

What is the moral to this story? If I hadn't been a homeschooler, none of it would have been possible. If my mom hadn't spent the time and loving care to help me harness my creative mind, I probably would have been a dropout. So to all of the homeschool parents out there, keep going! What you are doing is valuable. In fact, I can't think of anything more important than investing in the life and future of your children. . . . Do something special to say thank you to your mom and dad for the time they have poured into your life. That's the reason we made the . . . family comedy *Moms' Night Out*: to say thank you to my mom, my wife, and moms everywhere. After all we've put them through, they deserve to be told they are awesome! . . . Keep dreaming.[1]

My dear sisters, princess warriors in the faith who are also mothers, never stop learning to trust God as you help your creatives learn to harness their creative minds. Don't forget that Jesus "has blessed us in Christ with every spiritual (given by the Holy Spirit) blessing in the heavenly realm!" (Ephesians 1:3). Ladies, the answer really *is* Jesus.

And we [have seen and] know [by personal experience] that the Son of God has [actually] come [to this world], and has given us understanding and insight so that we may [progressively and personally] know Him who is true; and we are in Him who is true—in His Son Jesus Christ. This is the true God and eternal life.

1 JOHN 5:20, AMP

The answer is eyes on Jesus, the Word. I want you to know more than just what I think: I want you to *know* what Jesus has said. Teach your children to be yielded to Jesus, learning to trust, obey, and walk in His works prepared just for us to walk in, having fellowship with Him, moment by wonderful moment forever as He transforms us.

> And all of us, as with unveiled face, [because we] continued to behold [in the Word of God] as in a mirror the glory of the Lord, are constantly being transfigured into His very own image in ever increasing splendor and from one degree of glory to another; [for this comes] from the Lord [Who is] the Spirit.
>
> 2 CORINTHIANS 3:18

> But when Moses went in before the Lord to speak with Him, he took the veil off until he came out. And he came out and told the Israelites what he was commanded. The Israelites saw the face of Moses, how the skin of it shone; and Moses put the veil on his face again until he went in to speak with God.
>
> EXODUS 34:34-35

This tells us that the face of Moses shone from being in the presence of God. There's a story I have heard many times of a woman in Birmingham who attended a large women's Bible study in the late sixties. When she first came to the study, she did not yet know the Lord. She attended for many weeks and then one day gave her heart to the Lord. Later she told the other ladies she had shopped in many cosmetic shops trying to find the makeup that she thought all of the other women were wearing. Before she came to Christ, she thought that the only explanation for the glow on all their faces was that they were all using the same makeup. Shine, Jesus, shine!

When I was in my senior year of college, I attended a conference in Atlanta. One of the classes I attended was on true beauty. I don't remember all that the teacher said, but one thing was burned into my heart that day. She said, "Ladies, if you are not beautiful at age sixteen, it might not be your fault. Maybe you just had bad genes." Everyone had a good laugh. Then she said, "But if you are not radiant by age forty, it is your fault."

When I close my eyes, I can still see the radiant face of my dear ninety-seven-year-old mama. There was not a place on that sweet, holy face that was not wrinkled, but every morning when I walked into her bedroom the whole room seem to glow, and so did her face.

What do people see when they look at you? Do they see one who is being transformed into God's very own image?

Second Corinthians 3:18 says that we are transformed by degrees. It's a process as we behold the Lord through the Word of God.

My beloved cousin Pastor Mike McGinnis told me once, "Life is not a single journey; rather, it is a series of journeys from one pivotal moment to another."

First, our journey with God must impact us and change us, and then we will have something to say. And because we have something to say, we can pass it on to our children and our children's children with boldness.

I've had a life-transforming event, and I have been changed. You see, I am not what I shall be, but I am not what I was. Mom, be encouraged. Your children are not perfect and neither are you. There is one thing I know I did right as I raised my creative sons: I believed that the Lord could and would do what He had promised. Colossians 2:2-3 says, "This is what I have asked of God for you: that you will be encouraged and knit together by strong ties of love, and that you will have the rich experience of knowing Christ with real certainty and clear understanding. *For God's secret plan, now at last made known, is Christ himself.* In him lie hidden all the mighty, untapped treasures of wisdom and knowledge" (TLB).

Be encouraged in Christ. He is able. Remember, you matter to Him. He has a wonderful story to tell through your life. He also has a story to tell through each of your children. What will be the "but God" moments in your life? What will you have the joy of encouraging and inspiring your children to achieve?

ACKNOWLEDGMENTS

THIS BOOK WOULD NEVER have been written without the help of many. First, I want to acknowledge my dear husband, Hank, who repeatedly told me for more than two years that I needed to write a book. Thank you for loving me and praying for me throughout all this time writing.

Thank you, Glenda Massengale (my sounding board), for your constant encouragement, prayer, and friendship throughout the years. I've always been able to depend on you. We have to remain friends for life—because you know too much!

I want to acknowledge a group of ladies who met with me every week for months to encourage and challenge me in my writing. Thank you to Kerri Burson, Sarah Newman, Glenda Massengale, Kristen Beason, Stephanie Barnes, Pam Arnold, Liz Clayton, and Linda Haley for truly being my Aaron and Hur and holding my hands up.

> When Moses held up his hand, Israel prevailed; and
> when he lowered his hand, Amalek prevailed. But
> Moses' hands were heavy and grew weary. So [the other

men] took a stone and put it under him and he sat on it. Then Aaron and Hur held up his hands, one on one side and one on the other side; so his hands were steady until the going down of the sun.

EXODUS 17:11-12

I give special thanks to Pam Arnold, Liz Clayton, and Ashley Farlow for your willingness to be a part of this project, spending hours editing my work. You make me look good!

Thank you to my sons, Andy and Jon Erwin, for allowing me to share our journey as parent and children. I feel so honored to have been a part of God's handiwork. I stand in awe and praise Him for the joy of watching you become the men you have become.

Most of all I want to thank my wonderful Savior and Lord, Jesus. Without Him I would not have this story to tell.

NOTES

INTRODUCTION: DREAMS DO COME TRUE
1. *Moms' Night Out*, directed by Jon and Andrew Erwin (Birmingham: Erwin Brothers Entertainment, 2014).
2. John D. Garr, *Feminine by Design: The God-Fashioned Woman* (Atlanta: Golden Key Press, 2012), 5.

TIP 4: YOU ARE THE RIGHT MOM
1. Elisabeth Elliot, *The Shaping of a Christian Family* (Grand Rapids, MI: Revell, 2005), 99.
2. "Corrie ten Boom Quotes," Goodreads, accessed November 18, 2019, https://www.goodreads.com/author/quotes/102203.Corrie_ten_Boom.

TIP 6: WHOSE DREAM IS IT?
1. Max Lucado, *The Great House of God* (Nashville: Word Publishing, 1997), 39.

TIP 13: TEACH THEM TO VALUE OTHERS
1. "Lionsgate Signs Multi-Platform Film and Television First-Look Deal with the Erwin Brothers and Kevin Downes," August 9, 2018, accessed November 18, 2019, http://investors.lionsgate.com/press-releases-and -events/press-releases/2018/08-09-2018-220014766.
2. Leah MarieAnn Klett, "'I Can Only Imagine' Team Launches Faith-Based Movie Studio, Announces Four New Films," *The Christian Post*, March 29, 2019, accessed November 18, 2019, https://www.christianpost .com/news/i-can-only-imagine-team-launches-faith-based-movie-studio -announces-four-new-films.html.
3. Kingdom Launch Video, National Religious Broadcasters, March 27,

2019, Erwin Brothers Entertainment, https://www.facebook.com
/KingdomStoryCompany/videos/660711181029130/.

4. Ibid.

FOUNDATION 2: "ANY OLD BUSH WILL DO"

1. Major Ian Thomas, *The Saving Life of Christ* (Grand Rapids: Zondervan, 1961), 59.

FOUNDATION 3: RECOGNIZE "BUT GOD" MOMENTS

1. *Woodlawn*, directed by Jon and Andrew Erwin (Kevin Downes Productions, 2015).

ESSENTIAL 1: EMBRACE YOUR FAITH

1. Major Ian Thomas, *The Indwelling Life of Christ* (New York: Crown Publishing Group, 2006), 9.

ESSENTIAL 4: LIVE HOLY

1. Randy Alcorn, foreword to *Holiness: The Heart God Purifies*, by Nancy Leigh DeMoss (Chicago: Moody Publishers, 2005), 10.

ESSENTIAL 5: FIGHT THE DREAM KILLERS

1. *War Room*, directed by Alex Kendrick (Kendrick Brothers Productions, 2015).

ESSENTIAL 6: FIND POWER FOR LIVING

1. Dr. Bill Bright, "Have You Made the Wonderful Discovery of the Spirit-Filled Life?" Cru, accessed November 18, 2019, https://www.cru.org/us/en/train-and-grow/spiritual-growth/the-spirit-filled-life.html.

TOOL 8: BE ARMED FOR BATTLE

1. Philip Nation, "Spiritual Warfare: Real Struggle. Real Victory," *Bible Study Tools* (blog), accessed November 18, 2019, https://www.biblestudytools.com/blogs/philip-nation/spiritual-warfare-christ-s-victory-is-our-victory.html.

TOOL 10: GIVE GOD YOUR YES

1. Jon Erwin, quoted in "Mother's Day Tribute: Mom's Night Out Film," *Jimmy Larche Abiding in Him Devotional*, accessed January 9, 2020, jimmylarche.com/moms-night-out-film/#.